PEACE THROUGH AGREEMENT

Peace Through Agreement

REPLACING WAR
WITH
NON-VIOLENT
DISPUTE-RESOLUTION
METHODS

Gerald Rabow

New York
Westport, Connecticut
London

Library of Congress Cataloging-in-Publication Data

Rabow, Gerald.
    Peace through agreement : replacing war with non-
violent dispute-resolution methods / by Gerald Rabow.
       p.   cm.
    Includes bibliographical references (p.   )
    ISBN 0-275-93505-1 (alk. paper)
    1. Peace. 2. Arbitration, International. I. Title.
JX1952.R18   1990
341.5'2—dc20   89-71110

Library of Congress Catalog Card Number: 89-71110
ISBN: 0-275-93505-1

First published in 1990

Praeger Publishers, One Madison Avenue, New York, NY 10010
A division of Greenwood Press, Inc.

Printed in the United States of America

∞

The paper used in this book complies with the
Permanent Paper Standard issued by the National
Information Standards Organization (Z39.48-1984).

10 9 8 7 6 5 4 3 2 1

CONTENTS

PREFACE

My profession is systems engineering, and hence my proposals in this book on how to achieve peace reflect a systems engineering approach to problem solution. I need therefore to describe in this preface what systems engineering is, why systems engineering can make a contribution to the attainment of peace, and how I came to my conclusions on achieving peace.

Systems engineering consists of determining how to best combine available or possible components into a system which is to perform desired functions. Complex systems are usually beyond the detailed understanding of a single person, requiring the combination of knowledge of experts from many different fields, each of whom has more detailed knowledge of a component of the system. It is the task of the systems engineer to abstract (from the experts directly and/or from their writings) the information about each component which is crucial to combining them into the system, and then to manipulate this information so as to devise the best possible system. (In a complex project, there may be a hierarchy of systems and systems engineers, with a lower level system constituting a component of a higher level system.)

Systems engineering is mostly identified with physical systems, particularly large-scale systems (e.g., a space transport system or a telephone system), because it would be impossible to build such systems without it. Such systems are based largely on the application of mathematics and physical sciences, and hence engineers in general and systems engineers in particular must be proficient in these subjects. Even primarily physical systems have human interfaces whose consideration is a part of systems engineering.

On the other hand, there is nothing in the concept of systems engineering that limits it to primarily physical systems. We do not yet have a recognized profession of societal systems engineering, but it is possible to state how systems engineering as now practiced would have to be extended to apply to societal systems. Systems engineers would have to become sufficiently proficient in relevant social sciences so that they could make use of available expertise in social and political areas in order to propose modified societal systems that could be demonstrated to perform better than existing systems. One difference between physical and societal systems that societal systems engineers would have to take into account is that whereas in physical systems the engineers' clients are usually few and the system goals are more or less separated from the system design, in societal systems the clients may be the entire population, which would have conflicting goals whose resolution is intertwined with the system design.

The attainment of peace is a societal systems problem of obviously considerable difficulty and complexity. Societal systems engineering skill is hence required as part of the solution. The attempt at the systems engineering of peaceful coexistence is, of course, not limited to (physical) systems engineers acquiring the necessary familiarity with societal principles and practices. It could also be approached by someone in a societal profession such as diplomacy, international relations, political science, or dispute resolution, acquiring the necessary capability in the logic of systems design. In the present case, the systems engineering orientation came first, and this is undoubtedly reflected in the kind of book that has resulted.

Systems engineers are optimizers; they seek to achieve the best system possible, subject to the existing physical and resource constraints. War appears to be suboptimum, drastically so. But what is the system that needs to be reformed in order to eliminate war, and thereby gain the huge potential benefits from its elimination? We could, of course, take all of society as the system to be optimized. This approach would require addressing such considerations as poverty, freedom, justice, education, economics, and the environment, in addition to the elimination of organized violence. While an optimized society (in almost any sense) implies the absence of war, such a solution may be more complicated and take longer to achieve than we can afford. Since war fought with nuclear or other sophisticated weapons may well cause irreversible harm to society, greater priority should probably be given to eliminating war than to other societal improvements, and the problem of war elimination more narrowly defined than the optimization of society.

The narrower system whose adequate reform should be sufficient to eliminate war is the international dispute-resolution system. The problem then becomes how to replace, with a better system, our present system (or non-system) of war as the ultimate mechanism of resolving disputes between nations. The solution proposed here involves, when necessary, arbitration as the final step. It will be argued that such a system is workable and can eliminate war. It will further be shown that each side to a dispute can better achieve its goals through such a dispute-resolution system than it can through one which includes war-like means.

As a system, this book on achieving peace through agreement includes several main component concepts. One component is the theory of non-zero-sum games, which mathematically describes the kind of conflict which leads to war. The way the theory is normally stated, it is not very helpful in the achievement of peace. I have modified the theory into a more helpful "Cooperation Theory."

Mathematical theory about something as complex as societal behavior can take us only so far. Realistic non-zero-sum games could help citizens and experts better understand many of the ramifications of non-zero-sum situations, but the games we normally play are zero-sum games. I have devised, and included as a second component, non-zero-sum versions of the games Scrabble, bridge, and basketball.

A third component is the arbitration of major international disputes. Based on a review of negotiation, third-party intervention techniques, and a refutation of conventional wisdom that arbitration cannot be used when nations' vital interests are at stake, a scheme for arbitration of major international disputes is proposed.

I have been working to develop these component concepts for a number of years, and have published prior versions in three articles: "Arbitration as a Means for Resolving Major International Disputes" (Rabow 1987), "The Social Implications of Non-Zero-Sum Games" (Rabow 1988b), both in *IEEE Technology and Society Magazine,* and "The Cooperative Edge: New versions of Scrabble, bridge, and basketball help teach us the advantages of cooperation in play and real life" (Rabow 1988a) in *Psychology Today. IEEE Technology and Society Magazine* is the publication of the IEEE (Institute of Electrical and Electronic Engineers) Society on Social Implications of Technology, of which I am an active member. I have sought some practical experience in third-party dispute resolution techniques by becoming a mediator in my town's (Livingston, N.J.) Neighborhod Dispute Resolution Committee.

I hope to convince you in this book that peace is necessary and possible, and can be achieved by the type of logical and systems-oriented approach here presented.

PEACE THROUGH AGREEMENT

1

INTRODUCTION

BACKGROUND

We must and we can now eliminate war. Deplorable as war is, it once served a function: it was the ultimate means for resolving disputes between nations. Among nuclear powers, that capability is now gone. Since there can be no winner in a nuclear war, and possibly no survivors, nuclear war cannot serve as a means for resolving disputes. Alternative means for resolving disputes between nations are required. This book provides a plan for the peaceful resolution of such disputes. Although we know that nuclear war must never be fought, much of society's thinking is still based on the concept that war prowess is the key to success. Part of the problem is how to disentangle concepts related to winning by superior force from those related to achieving the best joint solutions among parties with conflicting interests.

Nuclear weaponry is thus forcing a replacement of the war system as our ultimate dispute-resolution mechanism, a change which we ought to be making anyway even where war might still be possible. While war, where usable as a dispute-resolution mechanism, can serve a function, this function comes at an extremely high price. That price is going up as weapons become ever more destructive, and as it becomes ever less possible to separate combatants from noncombatants. Almost any alternative that can be devised, even at substantial cost, should be vastly preferable.

Much progress has recently been made in our understanding of dispute-resolution techniques that could be used to resolve disputes which heretofore have led to war. Theoretical and experimental research has been done in negotiation, mediation, and arbitration. A branch of mathematics dealing with conflict, called (perhaps somewhat misleadingly) game theory, has developed. Examples where modern dispute-resolution techniques have successfully been applied to range from alternative dispute-resolution techniques in our court system to international negotiation. In alternative dispute resolution in the courts, disputes are typically resolved by agreements between the parties with the aid of a mediator. Examples of successful difficult international negotiations include the Law of the Sea treaty and the Camp David negotiations between Egypt and Israel.

Another useful advance is our increasing ability to understand and design large-scale, complex systems in general, and to see the world as a system in particular. Formulating a conception of a world that can function without war, and a way of getting from here to there is a problem in system design.

In this book a number of recommendations are made for actions that society should take to resolve disputes peacefully. Recommended actions depend on how one views, or models, society. One model might suggest that the way to achieve national objectives is through superior military capability. Another model might suggest that military strength can become irrelevant, and that the key to the well-being of all parties is agreement on conditions of fairness. Hence, a number of classical and novel models of conflict situations are examined in this book.

It turns out that society can indeed be modeled in a way that is consistent with peaceful resolution of disputes. It should be understood that society is neither static nor impervious to information about itself. Society models can be self-fulfilling. If leaders of nations believe that large military forces are essential to survival, then there will be large military forces, and defenseless nations probably will not survive. If, on the other hand, leaders of society believe disputes can be resolved peacefully, then they will invest in dispute-resolution capabilities, and with these capabilities resolve disputes.

Two actors who appear in all the conflict models are cooperators and defectors. Cooperators behave in such a way that when only cooperators participate in an encounter, they jointly obtain the best possible result (their total payoff is greatest). Defectors, called by that name because they defect from action that promotes the common good, try to take advantage of other participants in the encounter, and do not incur the risks necessary to cooperate with other participants for mutual gain. When only defectors participate in an encounter, their results are much poorer than the results of the cooperators when only cooperators participate in the encounter. Defectors are in some ways analogous to highly armed, belligerent nations. Cooperators are in some ways analogous to disarmed nations settling their disputes by peaceful means.

A crucial question is whether, and how, cooperators can protect themselves from defectors when both can participate in the encounter. This question extends from models of the simplest conflict games to models of international relations. We will find, in all those models, that the cooperators can indeed protect themselves from the defectors. The cooperators can adopt strategies so that it will not be to anyone's advantage to be a defector. Would-be defectors will be much better off by becoming cooperators. In consequence of this, it should be possible to devise a system whereby international disputes are settled by peaceful means. Such a system will be stable; it will not be in the interest of any nation to try to subvert the system.

What means of resolving international disputes shall replace war? It will be shown that arbitration appears to be the most expeditious mechanism for that task. As war must be rejected because it is no longer workable as a dispute-resolution method, so will arbitration be accepted as its most viable substitute. The scheme for arbitration suggested here is the one requiring the minimum adjustment from the present way of conducting international relations, as follows:

Nations will attempt to negotiate their differences, to the extent possible. Where they cannot agree but where a decision must be reached, they will frame the disagreement in such a way that an arbitrator can reach a decision. They will select an impartial arbitrator, itself a significant negotiation but generally simpler than negotiating the original dispute. The arbitrator's decision, once made, will be self-enforcing, because no side would accept less than the arbitrator's award, and both sides prefer any decision the arbitrator could make to a continuation of the dispute (which would formerly have led to war).

PLAN OF THE BOOK

The plan of the book is as follows:

Chapter 2 explains why war can no longer be used as a means for resolving disputes between nuclear powers. Scenarios are provided to show that nuclear weapons cannot be relied on to deter either nuclear war or conventional war. Nor is war safe even after nuclear disarmament; nuclear weapons can be reproduced. Nuclear-age confrontation is so full of paradoxes that the only safe alternative is to eliminate war and provide other means for resolving disputes.

Chapter 3 describes the state of the art of negotiation, mediation, and arbitration, which are tools for the peaceful resolution of disputes. To make arbitration applicable to the resolution of major international disputes, it must be modified so that arbitration decisions will be obeyed in the absence of external organs of enforcement. It turns out that this indicates the use of single-text mediation techniques as a component of the arbitration of major international disputes.

Chapters 4, 5, and 6 treat games that are sufficiently simple to examine mathematically, including the Prisoner's Dilemma and Dollar Auction. (To the mathematically timid: Don't worry. In the few places where mathematics is used at all as part of the discussion in this book, it never exceeds a basic high school level; readers who have forgotten even that should still be able to follow the discussion, provided they trust me to have handled the math correctly.)

Non-zero-sum games are simplified models of societal conflicts, and share with them the property that through cooperation, all participants can increase their payoffs. Understanding such games provides insights that are necessary to the better handling of societal conflicts. I will show that conventional recommendations on how to play these games do not call for sufficient cooperation, and that the more cooperative solutions I propose result in better outcomes for all the players.

Chapters 7 through 10 examine more complex games, which are too complex to solve mathematically but are challenging for people to play. Recreational games that are popularly played are almost all zero-sum games, in which one player's (or team's) loss is always exactly an opponent's gain, and hence these games do not provide good insight and experience for dealing with societal conflicts. I have therefore devised non-zero-sum versions of the games of Scrabble, bridge, and basketball; these modified games should be at least as interesting to play as the original zero-sum versions. The widespread playing of these non-zero-sum games would give the general population much-needed opportunities to experience non-zero-sum conflicts in a way in which strategy can be readily correlated with results. At the same time, the winning strategies that top-ranked tournament players evolved would provide further insight into appropriate ways of handling non-zero-sum conflicts.

In Chapter 11, I propose a theory of cooperation that is a generalization of the more cooperative (than those of previous analysts) solutions that I had proposed for the specific simple non-zero-sum games considered earlier. In contrast to the simple games, the choices which constitute cooperation in more general situations cannot usually be worked out independently by the participants, but require agreement by them as to how to define the overall welfare of the participants. Such agreement should be reached through research, negotiation, and/or arbitration. Once such agreements exist, cooperative strategies are superior in general non-zero-sum situations, just as they are in simple non-zero-sum games.

The scheme for arbitration of major international disputes is presented in Chapter 12. The scheme is consistent with the preceding material in the book: the absolute necessity of avoiding war, the state of the art of dispute resolution, the theory that cooperation is best and can overcome defection in all non-zero-sum situations, and the need to have questions of fairness that resist negotiation determined by arbitration. Arbitration is the best way of resolving problems that are otherwise unresolvable by peaceful means, but which must be resolved. The scheme provides for procuring the most competent and fairest arbitrators possible. Arbitration, and the arbitration decisions, will be accepted because everyone realizes that all alternatives would be worse for everyone.

Chapter 13 suggests steps we might take to get to the proposed state of world cooperation, where peace prevails because disputes are resolved through peaceful means. "Don'ts" would include: *don't* rely on excessive strength, *don't* put off negotiating. "Do's" would include: *do* agree on stopping environmentally damaging arms production, such as plutonium and tritium products for nuclear warheads; wherever verification is possible, *do* agree on stopping all research and development of new or improved weapons; *do* start making plans immediately for conversion from military to civilian production, to smooth the way for eventual disarmament. Individuals can help by learning and applying non-zero-sum principles, playing non-zero-sum games, and insisting that elected officials understand and utilize non-zero-sum principles. Supporting peace can be pleasant; peace supporters can use cooperative approaches in peace advocacy.

The Appendix provides a scenario of how arbitration might have prevented the U.S.–Vietnam war. The Notes provide not only references for statements in the text, but also some interesting sidelines, and so I hope you will not neglect them. The same goes for the Preface, which describes systems engineering and relates it to the solution of societal problems and the attainment of peace.

2

PARADOXES OF NUCLEAR CONFRONTATION

This book contended at the outset that war can no longer be used as the ultimate means for resolving disputes between nuclear powers. We will examine here the justification for that statement and some consequences.

Let us start out by postulating that full-scale nuclear war is not an admissible outcome. Almost everyone agrees on that. "Nuclear war cannot be won and must never be fought."[1] Let us hence exclude the option of deliberately using nuclear war to resolve a dispute between nuclear powers.

Could nuclear powers agree to conduct a limited war to decide a dispute between them? That does not make much sense. For one thing, such a war would not have the finality of conventional war of the past; the losing side could renege on accepting the peace terms demanded by the winning side, leaving the dispute still unresolved, with each side still with its nuclear weapons. For another, there is no assurance that the war would stay within the proposed limits and not escalate into full-scale nuclear war. Even if a disarmament treaty had previously eliminated all existing nuclear weapons, that would not necessarily prevent a war from becoming nuclear; the knowledge of how to make nuclear weapons would still be there, and weapons could be reproduced during the course of a war, or even when hostilities threaten.

The one advantage that war has had as a dispute-resolution mechanism in the past is that no agreement was needed; either side could initiate it, and the winning side could impose its terms. Limited war, by definition, does require agreement. With the advantage of decisiveness gone, war becomes a poor dispute-resolution mechanism indeed. If the disputants could agree on a neatly defined limited war, they should also be able to agree on some surrogate mechanism which would be much less horrendous than war and yet give each about the same chance of winning. However, as will be shown later, arbitration is a better alternative.

If war has been made useless as a decision mechanism for disputes between nuclear powers, do we need a decision mechanism at all? Why not just leave difficult disputes unresolved, trusting that each side's nuclear weapons will keep the other side from doing something rash? For the following reasons allowing disputes to fester is a bad and very precarious solution: In many disputes, the two parties are not equally dissatisfied with a current situation; one might be quite content with the status quo, while the other is determined to change it. The party desiring change might take some action to change it. The other makes an opposing move. The situation could escalate, with no guarantee of any stopping point.

The threat of a nuclear response may not suffice to deter one side (X) from taking incremental action against the other (Y). A threat to deter such action is itself deterred by the threat of a nuclear counter-response to any nuclear response to the original action. Once the original action has been taken, deterrence thereby having failed, it is not at all attractive to plunge the world into nuclear destruction by a nuclear response that could trigger a nuclear counter-response. Better to write off the deterrence plans. But if X thinks this is what Y will do, then there is no deterrence in X's original action. Hence, nuclear weapons cannot be relied on to deter a non-nuclear provocation. On the other hand, someone at some point may decide to carry out a nuclear response. (For example, the United States has not ruled out a nuclear response to a Soviet non-nuclear attack in Europe.) Likewise, a nuclear war may be initiated accidentally, especially during the increased tension of a crisis.

Nor are nuclear weapons even guaranteed to deter a nuclear attack. Consider the following scenario:[2] Country X has just launched a full-scale nuclear attack on country Y, which will destroy it. You are the leader of Y, and have the capability of initiating a counterstrike which will destroy X. Will you order that strike? With deterrence having failed and your country destroyed, or about to be, what purpose will it serve? Let's sharpen the scenario. The theory of nuclear winter[3] has been fully worked out by that time, and you have been informed that the attack on Y has been so calibrated that it alone will allow the earth to survive that phenomenon, whereas the addition of a strike on X sufficient to devastate it will wipe out all life on earth. Do you still order the strike, taking all that innocent life? As leader of Y, you must of course have said yes to that question all along, to try to make deterrence credible. But what will you do in the crunch, and what do the leaders of X think you will really do? If they do not believe that you will retaliate in such a case, then your nuclear weapons might not deter a nuclear attack.

Another paradox is that attempts to develop a defense against nuclear weapons are likely to make matters worse. Such thinking led to the signing of an ABM (Anti-Ballistic Missile) Treaty between the United States and Soviet Union in 1972, but the SDI (Strategic Defense Initiative, also known as Star Wars) program reopened consideration of providing a defense against nuclear ballistic missiles. It is now generally agreed that any foreseeable ballistic missile defense system cannot prevent a sufficient fraction of a full-scale Soviet nuclear attack from getting through to completely devastate the United States,[4] and in that sense would not change the basic nuclear confrontation. A partially successful missile defense system would, however, upset the present nuclear balance and trigger a new dimension of the arms race, including more nuclear missiles to make up for those likely to be intercepted, quick-boost missiles and other countermeasures, and means of attacking defense system components. Defense systems that mutually protect (or are believed to protect) against a second (attenuated) strike but not against a first (full) strike would be unstable and very dangerous, because they could tempt one nation to launch a surprise attack, depending on its defense system to protect against the remaining retaliatory capability of the other nation. If, on the other hand, one nation first developed an effective nuclear shield while still possessing offensive nuclear weapons, thus being able to threaten others with impunity, it would probably not be allowed to deploy it. If it tried, other nations would likely attempt to destroy such a shield, possibly triggering a nuclear war in the process.

That nuclear confrontation is so full of paradoxes means that we do not really understand it, much less want to depend on it to keep the peace. The sooner we dismantle this monstrosity, the better. But our aim should not be to make the world safe for non-nuclear war. One of the reasons we should not do so is that there is no assurance that non-nuclear war between superpowers will stay non-nuclear very long, even without initial stockpiles of nuclear weapons.

Neither nuclear deterrence, nor attempts at defense against nuclear weapons, nor the capability to fight non-nuclear war, are the right tools for attaining peace. What is needed is progress in non-violent ways of resolving disputes. We turn to that next.

3

NEGOTIATION, MEDIATION, ARBITRATION

This chapter describes state-of-the-art approaches to the peaceful resolution of disputes.[1] Subsequent chapters, especially Chapter 12, describe how these techniques can be extended to the resolution of major international disputes. Throughout this book, I will use the words "dispute resolution" rather than "conflict resolution." A dispute is a uniquely human phenomenon, whereas a conflict can occur throughout the animal and vegetable kingdom. A dispute is a difference of position on how best to deal with a conflict. It can be resolved through agreement.

The initial attempt to resolve a dispute is normally via negotiation among the disputing parties alone, and this is treated in Section I of this chapter. Most disputes are resolved this way. If unaided negotiations appear not to be succeeding, one of several methods involving an outside party, including mediation and/or arbitration, can be utilized. Such methods are described in Section II of this chapter.

I. NEGOTIATION

Negotiation is a process whereby, ideally, disputing (or potentially disputing) parties attempt to reach an agreement that satisfies the needs of each of them as much as possible. This generally involves an integrative and a distributive component. For example, a business partnership, if it can be properly organized, can earn more money than its members could otherwise earn individually. Agreement on what duties each partner should perform so as to maximize the income of the partnership constitutes the integrative component of the process. Agreement on how to divide the income among the partners constitutes the distributive component; equal division might not be appropriate if the skill levels of the partners differ significantly. The distinction between integrative and distributive components may not always be as clearcut as in this example.

Perhaps the best-known book on the negotiation of agreements is *Getting to Yes* by Fisher and Ury (1983). The authors recommend a method of "principled negotiation" consisting of "separating the people from the problem," "focusing on interests, not positions," "inventing options for mutual gain," and "insisting on using objective criteria." Each of these four principles is described below in the course of placing it as an integrative or distributive component of negotiation.

Integrative Component of Negotiation

The integrative component of negotiation requires that the parties consider the subject of the negotiation as a common problem that they need to solve cooperatively. There is therefore a need to concentrate on this problem, rather than letting the relationship with the other party or parties get in the way of cooperating to solve the problem. This is what is meant by separating the people from the problem. Negotiators should neither demand concessions on the issues as a condition for friendly relations, nor make such concessions in an attempt to buy friendship. Techniques that promote a good problem-solving relationship include imagining yourself in others' shoes; avoiding accusations; clarifying perceptions; understanding, explaining, and not escalating emotions; using appropriate symbolism; listening actively; and speaking purposefully.

Negotiators should focus on interests, not positions, because it is interests that the parties need to satisfy. To the extent that positions differ from interests, the problem solving that could occur to integrate the interests of the parties cannot occur when only positions are considered. The classic example is that of two children whose positions are that each wants as large a part as possible of an orange. It turns out, however, that the interest of one is in the juice, while the interest of the other is in the rind (for baking a cake). A much better solution to the division of the orange can obviously be attained knowing the interests than could be attained knowing only the positions. Basic human needs such as security, economic well-being, a sense of belonging, recognition, and control over one's life are often not fulfilled because negotiators are instead quibbling over narrower positions. The interests of all who have a stake in a negotiation should be represented, otherwise, those whose interests are not adequately taken care of may thwart any agreement.

In addition to understanding the interests of the various parties, it is necessary to synthesize a solution that, as much as possible, satisfies all those interests. This is facilitated by inventing options for mutual gain. One technique that can be used to get started is known as brainstorming. In brainstorming, a group of participants tries to think of, and record, as many approaches to a problem as possible; negative criticism is never allowed in this stage, but friendly, enhancing amendments are encouraged. Only subsequently are the ideas evaluated and the best selected for further development.

Another technique for achieving mutual gain is the identification of shared or dovetailing interests. It is also often helpful to divide the issues into many small elements, then examine various ways of combining the elements to see which ways mutually satisfy the interests of the parties. Where the number of possible combinations of elements becomes very large, computerized processes for identifying favorable combinations of elements might be considered.[2]

Negotiation to achieve mutual gain may be difficult in practice, but it is conceptually easy. The result of a perfectly accomplished process of integrative negotiation is referred to as Pareto optimality, named after Vilfredo Pareto. If an arrangement is Pareto optimal, there is, by definition, no way any party could get more (have its interests better satisfied) except by some other party getting less. This is just another way of saying no further integrative improvement is possible when the system is Pareto optimal. If there is only one Pareto optimal solution, or if the parties can discover only one (perhaps because they are exhausted by the time they reach it), then its discovery successfully completes the negotiation. Everybody has gained. A situation approaching this happy state of affairs is also referred to as a win-win solution: all parties have won in achieving their interests.

There is, however, usually more than one Pareto optimal solution. Then the parties must engage in distributive negotiation in order to decide which Pareto optimal solution to adopt.)

Distributive Component of Negotiation

In theoretical analyses of distributive negotiation, it is usually assumed that the parties are aware of the available Pareto optimal solutions, and that the negotiation is about which of these solutions to select. Each party can rank the available Pareto optimal solutions from most desirable to least desirable. When there are only two parties, it is easy to see that their rankings must be exactly in inverse order. (If some solution were less preferred by each, it would not be Pareto optimal.) The interests of the two parties in distributive negotiation are in this sense directly opposed. Because of this conflict, distributive negotiation is conceptually more difficult than integrative negotiation. An example in which the above model of distributive negotiation is approached is in negotiation about the sale price of a house. The seller of the house wants as high a price as possible, the buyer as low a price as possible. (Assume all possibly integrative considerations, such as whether to include the refrigerator, or when to move in, are insignificant or have been decided.)

The paradoxical phenomenon about distributive negotiation is that in the quest by each party to obtain the outcome most favorable to it, they may fail to reach an agreement at all. There is a best outcome that each party can obtain unilaterally in the absence of any agreement. This is called BATNA (Best Alternative To a Negotiated Agreement) by Fisher and Ury. The importance of being able to reach an agreement depends on the differences between the values of the BATNAs of the parties, and the values to them of the available Pareto optimal solutions. If the difference is small, then too much is lost by being unable to reach an agreement. It may happen, of course, that no agreement that gives each party at least as much as its BATNA is possible, and then no agreement should be reached. In the case of the house, for example, if the price the buyer can afford is less than the price at which the seller is willing to sell, there can be no deal. On the other hand, the value difference between possible agreements and BATNAs can be huge. Going to war rather than reaching an agreement is the most notorious example, and we know of course that this can happen.

How, then, can negotiators decide which of the available Pareto optimal solutions to adopt? They should use objective criteria for making such a selection, and insist that the other negotiators do likewise. If the parties propose differing criteria, then they must find some higher principles upon which they agree and from which objective criteria can be derived, or they must come up with some process through which a decision can be made. Mediation and arbitration are possible processes. The search for objective criteria to make a selection should be treated as a common problem that needs to be solved cooperatively, and hence the need and the techniques to separate people from the problem applies in this phase of negotiation as well as in the integrative phase.

Back to our house-sale example, the objective criterion that the parties might invoke is that the sale price should be consistent with that of other houses that have changed hands in the neighborhood. Differences between the houses that might affect their values would, of course, have to be carefully taken into account. An alternative criterion might be to split the gain from trade, that is, agree on a price halfway between the price at which the seller is indifferent between selling and his/her BATNA, and that similarly corresponding to the buyer's BATNA. That is probably an inferior criterion, because it is difficult for each party to verify the other's claimed BATNA. However, the two concepts might be combined. The parties might come out with differing calculations of how the prices of houses in the neighborhood should translate to the house in question. The differences in those calculations might be split.

In the sale of the house, splitting final differences may not be unreasonable, because buyer and seller can be presumed to be in roughly similar circumstances. That does not hold for all negotiations. When there are large asymmetries, the logic of splitting differences becomes very questionable, and suggestions for splitting differences should be approached with caution.

When the penalty of not reaching agreement is large, such as when the alternative is war, then the attainment of an agreement is of much greater importance than the precise nature of the agreement and which party gets slightly more or slightly less. Hence, it is important to remove obstacles to the reaching of an agreement, and to overcome calls for obtaining partisan advantage. This applies particularly where, as is usually the case in large-scale negotiations, the prime negotiating parties are not homogeneous entities, but are composed of factions which must define their negotiating interests in subsidiary dispute-resolution processes. The interests of all factions must be adequately attended to in the top-level negotiation, because otherwise the slighted factions might withhold consent that may be necessary for their party to conclude a top-level agreement. On the other side of the coin, in the subsidiary dispute-resolution processes, peace-loving factions should resist the adoption of positions that would endanger the peaceful resolution of a dispute in the top-level negotiation.

The material in this section has not been meant to be an exhaustive summary of negotiation techniques, but represents my interpretation of the best negotiation approaches that have come to my attention. The use of superior negotiation techniques should enhance the likelihood of negotiation success. However, negotiators are not perfect, and negotiations that ought to succeed sometimes fail. If the dispute is important enough to require settlement, disputing parties should then seek third-party help.

II. THIRD-PARTY INVOLVEMENT

If disputing parties cannot settle a dispute among themselves, then the only peaceful alternative for dispute settlement is to obtain the help of a third party (so-called even when there are more than two parties in dispute). Help from third parties can come in many forms, including the broad categories of mediation, arbitration, and judicial decision — mediation being the most voluntary of the three processes, and judicial process the least voluntary.

In mediation, the parties are not obligated to accept the suggestions of the mediator. The involvement of the mediator can vary widely, depending on the type of mediation used. At one extreme, the mediator might do no more than initiate communication between the disputing parties. At the other extreme, single-text mediation, the mediator might, after a thorough exploration of the situation, offer the disputing parties a proposed solution on a take-it-or-leave-it basis. Single-text mediation actually has much similarity to the scheme proposed in this book for the arbitration of vital interest international disputes, and hence will be presented below as a separate subsection, following those for mediation and arbitration.

Arbitration differs from mediation in that the arbitrator must reach a decision that is binding on the disputing parties.[3] However, the submission of a dispute to arbitration requires the consent of all the parties, at least at the time that agreement is reached (or bought into) that the parties will submit all disputes of a certain type to arbitration. This contrasts with the conventional judicial process, where a party may be required to submit to the jurisdiction of a court whether the party desires it or not. Additionally, arbitration procedures and the selection of arbitrators can be fashioned by the disputing parties to meet their particular needs, whereas judicial processes are much less responsive to the particular needs of specific disputants.

There has been a recent trend toward so-called alternative dispute resolution (ADR), including mediation and arbitration, as a replacement for judicial decisions in the courts. One motivation for this is to reduce the volume of work for the courts, but the ADR process can also result in a much more satisfactory resolution than the courts can provide. For example, when a party enters a court complaint against a neighbor, a decision by the court either does or does not impose a sanction on the defendant. If instead, the complaint is referred to a neighborhood dispute-resolution committee that provides mediation, a mediator (or a group of mediators) can help the parties find a mutually satisfactory solution to the dispute. It is very often found that the complaint filed with the court does not represent the real problem, and that once an accommodation to resolve the underlying problem can be worked out, the complaint can be withdrawn. In the small fraction of the cases in which mediation fails, the parties are free to take their complaints to court in the normal way. Other types of disputes in which ADR has proved useful include disputes involving corporations, public interest disputes, family and child custody disputes, malpractice and personal injury claims, and consumer disputes.[4] Of course, mediation and arbitration have long been used in labor-management disputes.

Mediation

Mediation is the inclusion in the negotiation process of an impartial "third" party who is knowledgeable in effective negotiation processes but has no power of compulsion to lead or assist disputing parties toward a favorable resolution of a dispute.[5] There are a number of reasons why mediation might succeed where unmediated negotiation is unsuccessful:

1. The mediator might, through training, experience, and/or natural ability, be more capable of negotiating than the negotiators for the disputing parties, and might be able to coach the negotiators to conduct the negotiation more effectively and hence more successfully.

2. The mediator might be able to obtain information from the disputing parties that they are

unwilling to reveal to each other. Having a more complete picture of the situation than any of the parties, the mediator thereby might be able to propose better solutions. A key to attaining such information from the parties is the assurance of confidentiality. Maintenance of strict confidentiality is a stock-in-trade of mediators.

3. Control of emotions by negotiators is an important element in successful negotiation. Inappropriate emotions are probably more easily recognized by someone other than the person having them. The mediator might therefore be able to recognize counterproductive emotions by negotiators and take steps to alleviate them. Similar reasoning applies to misperceptions of reality.

4. There are frequently indivisible alternatives, one of which is preferable to one party and a different one to another, with no obvious choice among the alternatives. In such a case, the mediator might make an explicit suggestion for, or implicitly nudge the parties toward, one of the alternatives. With the lack of any other means of making the selection, the mediator's choice becomes salient. It is the possibility of such a situation that makes (*a priori*) impartiality essential for mediators.

There is some debate among mediators as to whether mediators should merely assist the parties in reaching an agreement, or whether mediators should also try to influence the outcome of the negotiation toward what the mediator considers a fairer agreement, or one more likely to endure, particularly in support of a party that is at a disadvantage in the negotiation. Approaches range from focusing on the process of negotiation and leaving the substantive content as the exclusive domain of the parties to helping empower the underdog to reach fair agreements, according to the intervenor's values.[6]

I take the following position: To the extent that the mediator is *sure* (s)he understands the situation better than the disputants do and can accurately express the joint welfare of the disputants, the mediator should, as best (s)he can, try to obtain a result which maximizes that joint welfare. (The concept of maximizing joint welfare will be explored in detail in Chapter 11.) To the extent that the mediator is *not sure* of the above, (s)he should maintain impartiality, assist the parties in the negotiation process so as to maximize the chance for reaching agreement, and leave the substantive content to the disputing parties, who are presumably better informed about it.

Our main concern in this book is international disputes, and mediation can, and has, been applied to such disputes. Where we discuss in this book negotiation as a first step in resolving international disputes, both negotiation with mediation as well as unmediated negotiation, alone or in combination, are meant to be included. Mediation is, after all, enhanced negotiation.

Arbitration

When negotiation, with or without mediation, is unsuccessful, the next (and, we hope, final) step in the resolution of a dispute is some form of third-party decision. Arbitration has some attractive advantages in general over other forms of third-party decisions, and may be the only practical form for the resolution of major international disputes. In this introduction to arbitration, we need to distinguish between the scheme for arbitration of major international disputes, as proposed in Chapter 12, and current, conventional arbitration.

In comparison to the most common alternative, decision in a court of law, conventional arbitration has the following characteristics:

1. In arbitration, the disputing parties can select the arbitrator or arbitrators, whereas in a court of law they must accept whatever judge is assigned, and if a jury is used, have very limited influence on juror selection.

2. The parties can specify the way the arbitration is to be conducted and can set limits on the discretion of the arbitrator(s), whereas in a court of law, they must conform to the existing rules, as well as schedules and location of the court.

3. Whereas most court proceedings are open to public scrutiny, arbitration proceedings can be kept confidential.

4. Arbitration insulates the dispute from court proceedings. Courts will not consider a dispute that is subject to arbitration, and arbitration decisions cannot be appealed to the courts except in very unusual circumstances.

5. An arbitration decision can be entered in court records and be enforced as if it were an official court judgment.

In the scheme for international arbitration proposed in Chapter 12, characteristics 1 (arbitrator choice) and 2 (control of process) are of even greater importance, while characteristic 3 (confidentiality) might not be utilized, and characteristics 4 (precedence and non-appealability) are irrelevant. The significant difference, however, is in characteristic 5 (enforceability). The scheme of Chapter 12 requires acceptance of the arbitration decision by the disputing nations without recourse to any external organ of enforcement. No analog of enforcement of national court decisions via a nation's police power is postulated in the scheme for arbitration of major international disputes.

In conventional arbitration, with enforcement, the arbitrator can be sure that any arbitration decision that is within the rules for that arbitration will stick. The only additional constraints on the arbitrator are the arbitrator's professional ethics, and perhaps the need to be perceived as doing a good job, in order to receive future arbitration assignments. In the absence of external organs of enforcement, but with the need that an international arbitration be accepted, the international arbitrator of vital disputes is in a much more precarious position, with much greater constraint on what constitutes an acceptable decision. Because of the lack of enforcement capability, it turns out that many of the skills of mediators are required in the arbitration of major international disputes, and that this process is closer to single-text mediation than to conventional arbitration.

Single-Text Mediation

In single-text mediation (also referred to as one-text procedure, single negotiating text, and single text negotiating document), the mediator is the developer and custodian of a single text that is to eventually constitute the agreement among the parties. (There may be two, a few, or many parties.) Mindful that the agreement must ultimately be approved by all the parties, the mediator involves the parties intimately in the development of the text. Typically, the mediator tries to ascertain the needs and suggestions of all the parties with respect to the matter under consideration, and from that information prepares a first outline of a solution. This outline is then submitted to all the parties for criticism. Utilizing the response from the parties, the mediator prepares a second draft, including more details, and again submits it to the parties. This process is iterated, perhaps dozens of times. Finally, when the mediator feels (s)he cannot improve the text any further, (s)he submits it to the parties, with a statement something like, "This is the best I can do. It should be better for each of you than not reaching an agreement. You are not likely to get an agreement which gives any of you any more. Therefore, I advise that you all accept this text."

Well-known examples of single-text mediation are the Camp David agreements between Egypt and Israel in 1978, and the Law of the Sea Treaty negotiated over the decade ending in 1982.[7]

Single-text mediation differs in only one essential respect from the proposed scheme for arbitration of major international disputes, namely that the scheme of Chapter 12 mandates that the nations commit themselves *a priori* to the acceptance of the third party's ultimate text, thereby turning it into the binding decision of an arbitrator. In single-text mediation, on the other hand, each party has the option to accept or reject, hence the possibility that a principal party will reject the text and thereby prevent agreement.

In the case of the arbitration decision, as we will see, what will make the parties (nations) enter into an agreement to arbitrate, accept the eventual arbitration decision, and abide by that decision in the absence of any supranational means of enforcement, is that any alternative action would be worse for each nation. It is informed self-interest that results in adherence to the arbitration decision, and indeed makes the whole scheme work.

Could not the single-text mediation process come to the same proposed agreement as the arbitration decision, and would not the informed self-interest of all the parties then also require all parties to accept the same agreement? Yes it could, yes it would, but – – –. In the single-text mediation case, the current estimate of self-interest is *all* that compels acceptance. In the case of the arbitration scheme, there are *additional* inducements to accept.

For major international disputes, failure to reach a peaceful resolution is unacceptable. Hence, we should *not* give nations a license to reject a last-chance agreement. If nations have committed to the arbitration process, then refusal to abide by it would mean additional costs to the reneging nation in the form of universal condemnation for not keeping its solemn commitment, and for destroying the best available means for keeping the peace. This is in addition to choosing a course in the matter in dispute that the best consensus of mankind has established as inferior. Therefore, it is prudent to go with the alternative requiring *a priori* commitment, and provide the extra strings for our bow.

Achieving peace through proper management of informed self-interest requires, in addition to the practical dispute resolution techniques just examined, an analytic and experimental understanding of conflict and disputes. The next eight chapters are concerned with that.

4

INTRODUCTION
TO GAME THEORY

Game theory is that branch of mathematics that deals with conflict of interest. It is a relatively recent branch, generally considered to have begun with Von Neumann and Morgenstern's book *Theory of Games and Economic Behavior* (1944, 1947). (A standard reference to game theory is *Games and Decisions* by Luce and Raiffa.[1]) Since conflicts among humans are generally too complex to model precisely, simplifying assumptions have to be made in order to treat such conflicts mathematically. The usefulness of the theory in helping with real conflicts depends to a large extent on how appropriately such conflicts are modeled.

The process begins with expressing the conflict as a game. A "game" connotes rules that are fixed and known to all participants, referred to as players, and quantifiable objectives for each player known to all other players. Such a game may be one of many existing games that humans play for recreation or for enhancement of skills, or may be one that has been especially designed to mimic some aspect of human conflict. It is very often necessary to make further simplifying assumptions in order to analyze games mathematically.

One such simplification is to put a game into "normal" form. Here, a player is assumed to have a "strategy," namely the decision this player would make at each possible situation in the game requiring a decision by this player. That could consist of either an enumeration of all such situations (often not practical because the number of possible situations is too great), or some formula or algorithm based on the significant parameters of the situation. When the strategy of each of the players is known, then the course of the game, and hence its outcome, is determined. This is true for each set of strategies of the players. Hence, the game can be described in normal form as a matrix of outcomes for each combination of the possible strategies of all the players.

The game objective can be expressed in terms of a satisfaction quantity, or "utility." In contrast to, say, a unit such as the dollar, where the millionth dollar may be of less significance to a recipient than the first dollar, an additional unit of utility is always assumed to be valued equally by the recipient. If the outcome is expressed in probability terms, then the recipient is assumed to value equal expected quantities of utility equally. (Expected value of any measure is defined as the sum of the products of the various possible values of the measure times the probability of attaining that value.) Game payoffs are generally presumed to have this utility property, and game players are presumed to desire to maximize their expected utilities. In order to model real situations as accurately as possible in games, utility must include all the satisfaction of participants in the real situation; in particular, it should include any satisfaction that a participant derives from the prospering of others, including family, friends, and society in general.

An important consideration in game playing is whether the game is zero-sum or non-zero-sum. In a zero-sum game, the sum of the payoffs to all the players is always the same. This payoff sum can always be made zero without altering the game, hence the name zero-sum for such a game. In a non-zero-sum game, on the contrary, the sum of the payoffs to all the players is not always the same, hence there is a possibility that the players can all gain by coordinating their strategies. Almost all commonly played recreational games are zero-sum. When war is modeled as a game, it is usually as a zero-sum game. On the other hand, most real-life encounters are non-zero-sum; here cooperation can improve the outcome for all the participants.

Two Person Zero-Sum Games

Games are also classified according to the number of players. Games are easiest to describe and analyze when there are only two players, and of those the simplest are zero-sum games. Game theory analysis hence begins with two-person zero-sum games.

An illustrative two-person zero-sum game in normal form is depicted in Figure 4-1. Player X can play x_1, thereby selecting row 1, or x_2, thereby selecting row 2. Similarly, player Y can play y_1, thereby selecting column 1, or y_2, thereby selecting column 2. Each selection must be made before that of the other player is revealed. The payoff is at the intersection of the selected row and column, the first entry being the payoff to X (the row selector), the second that to Y. The fact that the two payoffs at each intersection sum to zero indicates that this is a zero-sum game. (Alternatively, if the game is specified to be zero-sum, only the first (X) payoff needs to be entered at each intersection). If, for example, X plays x_1 and Y plays y_2, then the payoff to X is 2 and to Y is -2. The set of all payoff numbers, depicted in Figure 4-1, is known as the payoff matrix.

	y_1	y_2
x_1	0 , 0	2 , -2
x_2	4 , -4	1 , -1

FIGURE 4-1. Zero-Sum Game Payoff Matrix

The solution to this game, arrived at by game theory, is for player X to play x_1 with probability 0.6 and x_2 with probability 0.4, and for Y to play y_1 with probability 0.2 and y_2 with probability 0.8, yielding an expected payoff of 1.6 to X and -1.6 to Y. (The payoff to X is $(0.6)(0.2)(0) + (0.6)(0.8)(2) + (0.4)(0.2)(4) + (0.4)(0.8)(1)$.) This strategy, of making random selection from among the pure strategies (x_1 and x_2, and y_1 and y_2, in the example) with chosen probabilities, is known as a mixed strategy. The payoff of 1.6 is the maximum payoff that player X can obtain when Y employs the best counterstrategy, and similarly -1.6 is the best payoff for Y. In this particular example, it can be seen that when X uses the indicated mixed strategy, the payoff is 1.6 to X regardless of Y's strategy, and vice versa. No other way could X ensure him/herself a 1.6 payoff; for example, if X always played the pure strategy x_2, then if Y played y_2, X would receive only 1.

The results of the example have been shown to hold generally for two-person zero-sum games with a finite number of pure strategies: There is a value of the game that each player can obtain with an appropriate mixed strategy (which in special cases could be a pure strategy).[2] Such a pair of strategies is known as an equilibrium pair. If one player, say X, deviates from equilibrium strategy, then Y might be able to take advantage by also deviating, but such deviation by Y might be risky, because X may be trying to lay a trap for Y. Hence, although a player should use an equilibrium strategy against a sufficiently good player, it is less clear what to do against a poorer player.

Two-Person Non-Zero-Sum Games

While there is general agreement on how a two-person zero-sum game should be played, at least against a good player, analysts differ on how two-person non-zero-sum games should be played, depending on what assumptions the analyst wishes to make.[3] Unfortunately, the mindset of most analysts is greatly influenced by the results from zero-sum games. In zero-sum games, the objective is to protect yourself from the most damaging strategy your opponent can use, since it is always in your opponent's interest to use it. Carrying this over to non-zero-sum games, analysts look first at protective strategies. Only if it is clearly in the other player's interest not to use the most damaging strategy, will these analysts recommend that you use a strategy that yields both of you a better payoff. The search stops for each player with the decision pair giving each player the largest payoff against the most damaging strategy of the other player that that player does not clearly prefer not to use. This is not necessarily a Pareto optimal outcome.

Pareto optimality is that condition where there is no other outcome that leaves somebody better off and nobody worse off.

It is a thesis of this book that the above approach to non-zero-sum games is undesirable, since the significant determinant of outcome is therewith the threat that one player can hold over the other. The alternative here favored is to start with the set of Pareto optimal outcomes (which the players desire to reach), decide which of these is most equitable, and devise strategies that will make it mutually undesirable to deviate from the favored outcome. In other words, instead of starting with an assumption of mutual antagonism and then seeing to what extent it can be mitigated, it is proposed to start with an assumption of cooperation, and to realize it by making defection unprofitable. The results of the two approaches are not the same. The two approaches will be examined for a number of classical non-zero-sum games in this and the following two chapters; both will be discussed further, and the cooperative approach extensively developed throughout the book. Where cooperative approaches are considered, the players are referred to as "partners" rather than "opponents."

Threat Game

A threat game is depicted in Figure 4-2. It is a 2 x 2 game, each player having two choices. X selects row 1 by playing x_1 or row 2 by playing x_2; Y selects column 1 by playing y_1 or column 2 by playing y_2. The intersection of the selected row and column indicates the payoffs to X and Y, the first entry being the payoff to X and the second that to Y. Thus, if X plays x_2 and Y plays y_1, the payoff to X is –1 and to Y is –200. The sum of the payoffs to X and Y is different for different choices, hence this is a non-zero-sum game.

	y_1	y_2
x_1	0 , 100	100 , 0
x_2	-1 , -200	-40 , -300

FIGURE 4-2. Threat Game Payoff Matrix

Classical, that is threat-based, analysis of this game is as follows: For a single play of this game, X prefers x_1 for any choice of Y, and Y prefers y_1 for any choice of X, so the result will be X plays x_1 and Y plays y_1, with payoffs of 0 for X, and 100 for y. However, if there is pre-play communication in which enforceable agreements can be made, the situation is different, because X can threaten to play x_2 unless Y commits to playing y_2. If agreement is not reached, causing X to carry out the threat, X's payoff is reduced only to -1, while Y's payoff will become -200. The game has turned into a bargaining game, where the result of no agreement is payoffs to X,Y of $-1,-200$, and the bargaining is over the probability of x_1y_2 (shorthand for X plays x_1, Y plays y_2) as contrasted to x_1y_1, if agreement is reached. For x_1y_2, X gains 101 and Y gains 200 with respect to the no-agreement point. For x_1y_1, X gains 1 and Y gains 300. For x_1y_2 with probability p and x_1y_1 with probability $1-p$, X gains $1+100p$ and Y gains $300-100p$. The classical (Nash) bargaining solution in the range of possible probabilities (i.e., $p=0$ to $p=1$) is $p=1$, that is, the pure result X plays x_1 and Y plays y_2, since according to the Nash bargaining solution, the product of the X and Y gains should be maximized. (The Nash bargaining solution is further described in Note 2, Chapter 11.)

If there is no pre-play communication, but the game is played repeatedly, then the same results can be obtained as with pre-play communication. X intermittently plays x_2 until Y gets "the message" to play y_2. Play might ultimately settle down to x_1y_2.

The cooperative solution, recommended in this book (and justified in later chapters), is for X to always play x_1, and for Y to alternate playing y_1 and y_2 (iterated game) or to play a mixed y_1y_2 strategy (single game with pre-play communication). With the apparent symmetry of the x_1y_1 and x_1y_2 payoffs of Figure 4-2, the probabilities of x_1y_1 and x_1y_2 should be equal. X can then deter Y from shortchanging X by being prepared to play x_2, and Y should not respond to any threats by X for a greater payoff than indicated above. Any deterring action should be no greater than necessary to make defection unprofitable. For example, if Y insists on invariably playing y_1, play of x_2 by X with a probability somewhat greater than 1/6 would be sufficient to make it unprofitable for Y to deviate from even probability of x_1y_1, x_1y_2. (Y's cooperative payoff averages 50; Y's payoff from $(5/6)(100) + (1/6)(-200)$ is also 50). When players play cooperatively, play depends only on fairly apportioning Pareto optimal payoffs, and threat payoffs are irrelevant.

Game of Chicken

The original game of Chicken consists of two drivers approaching each other head-on at high speed. The driver who veers away first (and successfully) is "chicken"; the other driver "wins" the game. If neither driver veers away successfully then there is a CRASH. The game can be represented as shown in Figure 4-3, where x_0 and y_0 represent continuing straight, x_1 and y_1 veering away first, 1 the utility of "winning," 0 the utility of "chicken," and -1000 the utility of CRASH. (Unlike the way the Chicken game is sometimes presented,[4] $x_1 y_1$ (both veering away) is not a valid result here; a determination, if necessary by electronic instrumentation, is made of who was first to veer away). Less frivolous application of the Chicken game is possible; for example, x_1 or y_1 can represent the first concession in a negotiation that would deadlock and eventually break up in the absence of such a concession.

	y_0	y_1
x_0	$-1000, -1000$	$1, 0$
x_1	$0, 1$	

FIGURE 4-3. Game of Chicken Payoff Matrix

Hawkish analysts have advised playing the game in the following manner:[5] If you want to play Chicken, and you want to win, attract the other player's attention, and in full view of that player, yank out the steering wheel and throw it away. Knowing that you cannot veer, the other player now has no reasonable choice but to veer away, and so you win.

I leave it as an exercise for the reader to determine what happens when both players employ this strategy.

This book's recommendation is that two cooperative players should use some fair division mechanism to decide which player should make the move (e.g., veer away) first. If the game is iterated, x_1 and y_1 should alternate. If there is pre-play communication, then a fair mechanism for the initial game can be agreed on, such as a coin-flip or arbitration. (In the negotiation version of Chicken, a mechanized random solution such as coin-flip may not be workable because the situation may not be obviously symmetrical, and the degree of asymmetry may be in dispute, leaving arbitration as the recommended mechanism.) If there is no pre-play communication, then some implicit mechanism should be used for the first game. Each player could veer away at some randomly determined time during the available time interval, where the interval may not extend beyond the point where a collision can be safely avoided. Non-cooperation can be deterred. For example, if X always played x_0, a y_0 with probability of 0.0005 would be sufficient to give X a smaller payoff than with cooperative play. In the absence of such a need for deterrence, neither player should ever hold off on veering away long enough to incur even a small probability of a CRASH result, regardless of the play of the other player.

The above examples, Threat Game and the game of Chicken, show how ideological assumptions about how non-zero-sum games should be played — defensively based on mistrust or cooperatively in search of mutual advantage — can affect the strategy that the players employ. The results tend to be self-fulfilling. Defensive players find their mistrust justified by their opposite's play, while cooperative players find their cooperation reciprocated. The above games are not the most extreme examples of how classical defensive approaches to non-zero-sum games can come to grief. In the following two chapters, the games Prisoner's Dilemma and Dollar Auction are presented, respectively, at greater length. These games are notorious for eliciting mutually disadvantageous outcomes. Additional game theory topics are presented in subsequent chapters. Coming attractions include discussions of the n-person game in the section of Chapter 11 titled "Downplaying of Coalitions," the Nash bargaining solution in Note 2, Chapter 11, and incentive compatibility in Note 3, Chapter 11.

5

PRISONER'S DILEMMA

The Prisoner's Dilemma (PD) is a widely studied game[1] that illustrates much that is wrong with current approaches to non-zero-sum situations, but also provides some clues on how to handle such situations better. The game is named after a situation in which two prisoners are enticed to incriminate each other, whereas they would be much better off if both remained silent. More generally, in this game the choice C (cooperate) always gets a player a lower score than the choice D (defect), but if the two players both choose C, then they each obtain a higher score than if both choose D. The game is fully explained in Section I of this chapter.

Two versions of PD are of special interest, namely the Single-Shot PD, and the Iterated PD. The conventional analysis for Single-Shot PD has recommended that both players defect; this is explained in Section II. On the other hand, a particular cooperative strategy

TIT FOR TAT has been found best for Iterated PD; this is described in Section III. There has been some confusion about a good strategy for Iterated PD when noise is present, for example, when player's play can change randomly from that which was intended; this is treated in Section IV. Finally, in Section V, issue is taken with the conventional recommendation that both players should defect in Single-Shot PD. It is contended that a cooperative TIT-FOR-TAT-like strategy should be adopted for all versions of PD, including Single-Shot PD.

I. PD GAME DESCRIPTION

A Prisoner's Dilemma (PD) game payoff matrix is shown in Figure 5-1. Each of two players, X and Y, makes a choice C or D, before the choice of the other player is revealed. If both make the choice C, each player receives a score of 3, or 3 units of value. When the players both choose C, the total payoff to the two players combined is highest, hence the designation "cooperate" for this choice. However, the game has been designed to make it difficult for the players to attain this cooperative result. For any choice by one player (say X), the other player (Y) can do better by defecting than by cooperating. For x_c (X makes the choice C), y_c yields 3 to y and y_d yields 5 to Y; for x_d, y_c yields 0 to Y and y_d yields 1 to Y. But if both players choose D, they obtain the payoff 1,1, worse than the 3,3 they could have obtained by both playing C. Therein lies the dilemma.

The anecdote that gives the Prisoner's Dilemma its name is as follows: Two prisoners were believed to have committed a crime for which the normal jail sentence is five years, but in order to convict them the District Attorney (DA) needed at least one to confess to

	y_c (Cooperate)	y_d (Defect)
x_c (Cooperate)	3,3	0,5
x_d (Defect)	5,0	1,1

FIGURE 5-1. Prisoner's Dilemma Payoff Matrix

the crime and implicate the other. Without this testimony, the DA could only get them on a lesser charge worth two years in jail. The DA therefore separated the prisoners and made each of them the following proposition: "If you confess, and your partner does not, I'll let you off free (instead of the two years I could always get you for). And if your partner confesses, I'll still give you a break — four years if you confess as against five if you don't. So you see, no matter what your partner does, you're better off confessing." Note that this situation is depicted by Figure 5-1, with the payoff matrix representing the number of years saved from a five-year jail sentence. Cooperate here means cooperating with the other prisoner and remaining silent, and defect meaning confessing and ratting on the other prisoner.

Figure 5-1 is one example of a payoff matrix constituting a Prisoner's Dilemma; the PD is more generally defined by Figure 5-2. The payoff R is the "reward" for each player when they both cooperate. P is the "punishment" payoff for each player when they both defect. Payoff T is the "temptation," obtained by a defecting player while the other cooperates. In turn, the player who cooperates while the other defects obtains "sucker's" payoff S. In order for the dilemma to operate, reward must be greater than punishment, sucker's payoff must be less (worse) than punishment, and temptation must be greater than reward. This is written mathematically as $T>R>P>S$. In addition, the sum of the reward payoffs to the two players must be greater than the sum of the temptation and sucker's payoffs, as otherwise the players, on the average, would do best by one playing C and the other D, a form of cooperation counter to the intent of the game. This restriction is written mathematically as $2R>T+S$. (The reader can verify that the matrix of Figure 5-1 meets all the above conditions.)

To summarize, no matter what one player plays, the other will do better by playing D than by playing C ($T>R$ or $P>S$), but both playing C gets each more than both playing D ($R>P$).

		y_c (Cooperate)	y_d (Defect)
x_c	(Cooperate)	R,R	S,T
x_d	(Defect)	T,S	P,P

FIGURE 5-2. Prisoner's Dilemma Payoff Matrix

II. CONVENTIONAL ANALYSIS OF SINGLE-SHOT PD

In the Single-Shot version of PD, two players play the game only once. Analysts are (reluctantly!) fairly unanimous in the conclusion that the only logical solution for both players is to play D, and that we are condemned to suffer the punishment payoff. The reasoning is as follows:

1. Your choice can have no influence on the other player's choice, since once your choice is known to that player, you two never play again. Hence, you base your response solely on how to respond to the independent choice of the other player.
2. If the other player's choice is D, your payoff is greater if you play D than if you play C.
3. If the other player's choice is C, your payoff is greater if you play D than if you play C.
4. There is no need to try to determine (if you could) the other player's choice, since your response would be the same regardless of the choice of that player or your knowledge of that choice.
5. For either choice (C or D) of the other player, you should play D because your payoff in either case will be greater than if you play C.

I now add that this seemingly impeccable logic is wrong. However, before revealing why in Section V, I want to cover in its proper historical time position the Iterated Prisoner's Dilemma, for which cooperation has been found to succeed.

III. ITERATED PD

In the Iterated Prisoner's Dilemma, two players play the PD game of Figure 5-1 or 5-2 repeatedly, with both players at each stage knowing the results of all previous play. Each player must now consider not only the effect of a move (the choice of C or D at a particular stage of the game) on the immediate payoff, but the effect of such a move on future moves of the other player. Needless to say, it is to the advantage of each player to get the other player to play C as much as possible.

The main topic of this section is long games, having many iterations, with the ending indefinite. Let us, however, briefly consider one more dilemma for conventional analysts, namely games of finite length. On the last move of such a game, the reasoning of the previous section would persuade both players to play D, since there is no future move to influence. But if both players are sure to play D on the last move, then play on the next-to-last move cannot influence future play, so both players play D on the next-to-last move also. By repetition of this reasoning all the way to the first move, both players play D each move for the entire game.[2]

A breakthrough in the Iterated Prisoner's Dilemma occurred when Robert M. Axelrod, a political scientist at the University of Michigan, conducted computer tournaments of various Iterated PD strategies.[3] Axelrod conducted two such tournaments, in which he invited experienced game theorists and others to submit computer programs for Iterated PD strategies to be played round-robin with each other, to see which would emerge with the highest total score over all the matches. The payoff matrix of Figure 5-1 was used. At each move, a strategy must specify the move C or D, having available to it all previous moves made by the partner strategy. (Recall that in non-zero-sum games, appropriate terminology is playing *with partners,* not *against opponents*).

One of the strategies entered into the tournaments was TIT FOR TAT, submitted by Anatol Rapoport, a psychologist and philosopher from the University of Toronto. The TIT FOR TAT algorithm was to play C on the first move; thereafter do whatever the other player did on the previous move. This was the simplest program submitted (and hence serves as a convenient example of a strategy). It also turned out to be by far the best strategy, and its success is perhaps the most important result to emerge from the tournaments. In the first tournament, 14 entries were submitted, to which Axelrod added a strategy RANDOM, which randomly played C or D with equal probability. Each of the 15 strategies played a match with every strategy, including itself, for five games of 200 moves each. The score for each strategy was the sum of the scores from all the 200x5x15 = 15,000 moves of each strategy, the score for each move determined according to the matrix of Figure 5-1.

The second tournament differed from the first in the following ways: The field (and hence the number of matches played by each) was larger, consisting of 62 entries, plus RANDOM. Each of the contestants in the second tournament was fully informed of the results of the first tournament, including Axelrod's extensive analysis. Finally, to preclude possible profit by contestants varying strategy near the end of the game, the length of each game was determined by a random drawing from an exponential distribution of median length 200. The lengths of the 5 games, not revealed to the contestants, were respectively 63, 77, 151, 156, and 308 moves.

The clear winner of the tournaments was TIT FOR TAT. TIT FOR TAT won both tournaments, five of six hypothetical tournaments also run by Axelrod (and came in second in the remaining one), and was the best-growing strategy in an ecological simulation in which the number of entries of each strategy in each succeeding tournament was proportional to the total score of those entries in the preceding tournament. The success of any strategy depends on the characteristics and numbers of other strategies entered in the tournament; the hypothetical tournaments were variants of the original tournaments with different weightings of participating strategies.

Why did TIT FOR TAT do so well? Axelrod attributes this to four characteristics of TIT FOR TAT, namely niceness, forgiveness, provocability, and clarity. Nice is defined as never being the first to defect, hence any nice strategy playing another nice strategy will cooperate on every move, getting the highest possible combined score. Being nice appears to be essential for success; all 8 of the top ranking entries of the first tournament were nice, as were 14 of the 15 top entries in the second tournament (the remaining top entry ranked eighth).

Being forgiving is needed to prevent minor episodes of defection from becoming permanent. TIT FOR TAT is forgiving, since a single move of cooperation by partner will cause TIT FOR TAT to again cooperate.

Being provocable is necessary to prevent being taken advantage of by other players. TIT FOR TAT promptly retaliates when tested by partner, which often convinces partner to cease defecting.

Clarity is a necessary adjunct to provocability. If retaliatory behavior is not recognized as such, then it will not deter the partner from continuing to defect. TIT FOR TAT is clear since it immediately responds to a defection, as well as to a resumption of cooperation.

It is interesting to note that the score that TIT FOR TAT got in any game was not, and could not be, higher than that of partner; it was either the same or slightly lower. TIT FOR TAT won through its success in getting partner to cooperate to enable both to get a high score.

The results do not establish that TIT FOR TAT is the best strategy, only that good strategies need to have

TIT-FOR-TAT-like qualities. Later studies have indicated that variations of TIT FOR TAT can perform better.[4] Such a strategy might passively test whether it was encountering a RANDOM strategy, and if so, switch to an all-D mode.

The success of TIT FOR TAT was a surprise to a great many people. It had not generally been predicted by analysts (only Rapoport submitted this strategy). Also indicative of the reluctance in society to recognize the necessity of cooperation is that there were 23 non-nice entries out of the total 62 entries in the second tournament, in spite of the explanation the entrants had received regarding the results of the first tournament, including the importance of being nice.

IV. NOISY ITERATED PD

A purpose of this section is to indicate that TIT FOR TAT strategies must be extended with care in situations in which the conditions of Axelrod's tournaments do not apply, but that they can be so extended. One of the conditions of the tournaments was that the submitted strategies were executed in the computer without error, and that the records of the past games were always correctly presented to all contestants. We know, of course, that errors do occur in the real world, and that strategies that are to be useful in the real world must be able to cope successfully with such errors. This kind of disturbance from error-free performance is referred to as noise. The way TIT FOR TAT is defined in the previous section, it is quite vulnerable to noise. For example, when both players intend to play TIT FOR TAT, a single inadvertent (noise-caused) change from C to D by one player causes the other to respond with a D on the next move, which is in turn reciprocated by the first player, causing both players to alternate C and D moves, out of phase. If, in this state, either player makes another inadvertent change from C to D, then both players will play D on every move thereafter (unless noise causes inadvertent change from D back to C).

The effect of such noise will be much less catastrophic if the definition of TIT FOR TAT is changed to the following: Play D if the number of times your partner has played D previously exceeds the number of times you have played D previously; otherwise play C. Note that in the absence of noise, both definitions lead to identical play, because a D play by TIT FOR TAT's partner always puts partner exactly one D play ahead of TIT FOR TAT, and a C play by partner always balances the count. (The new TIT FOR TAT version could be mechanized with the aid of a difference counter, which in the noisefree case only attains counts of 0 and 1). With partners who both use the modified version of TIT FOR TAT in a noisy environment, an inadvertent D TAT is followed by a single D TIT by partner, after which cooperative play resumes. The need for modifying the TIT FOR TAT definition in a noisy environment has not been fully appreciated in the literature, and this has caused undeserved criticism of TIT FOR TAT.[5]

Even the modified TIT FOR TAT strategy is not the ultimate in TIT FOR TAT strategies in a noisy environment. Partners playing TIT-FOR-TAT-like strategies with each other in a symmetrical noise environment could obtain higher scores by not immediately responding with an intentional D TIT to an unintentional, noise-caused D TAT by partner, but instead waiting for a noise-caused D TAT to balance the D count, thereby reducing the total number of D occurrences. There is then the question of how far to fall behind in the D count before intentionally responding with D. Greater leeway results in better scores in matches between truly cooperative partners, since the number of D moves is minimized, at the cost of a lower score with an opportunistic partner who tries to sneak in as many extra D moves as conditions allow.

The strategy suggested for noisy environments is a TIT FOR STAT strategy (TIT FOR STATISTICAL TAT), namely to respond with a D TIT when it is statistically likely that partner intentionally played D when an appropriate TIT FOR STAT strategy would have required playing C. There is tradeoff on how high the probability of violation should be before a D response is made; a higher probability results in a better score in games between TIT FOR STAT partners, but a lower score for a TIT FOR STAT player with partner attempting a statistically innocuous increase in D moves. If the noise is small, for example, the probability of an inadvertent change from C to D is small, then the precise threshold used is not very important; with any reasonable threshold, the reduction in score for a TIT FOR STAT player would be small both with a TIT FOR STAT partner and a partner who merely wants to appear to play TIT FOR STAT. In a noisefree environment, TIT FOR STAT becomes identical to TIT FOR TAT.

TIT FOR STAT is applicable to errors in the presentation of each other's move to the players, as well as to noise-caused changes of intended move. The players (or the designers of computerized strategies) must, however, have some sort of information about the likelihood of errors that can occur. Since the rules of the Axelrod tournaments implied a noisefree environment, it would not be fair to criticize the strategies as submitted there for their performance in a noisy environment.

V. THE CASE FOR COOPERATION IN ALL VERSIONS OF PD

While the case for playing C on the first move of a long sequence of Prisoner's Dilemma is now widely accepted due to the result of Axelrod's tournament that it pays to be nice (never be the first to defect), analysts still maintain that the "rational" play in Single-Shot PD is to play D.[6] We will now see why it is not correct to always defect in Single-Shot PD, and how TIT FOR TAT can be extended to apply to all versions of PD, Single-Shot and short-length repeated PD as well as long length Iterated PD.

Defects of Defection in Single-Shot PD

A way of rephrasing the reasoning of Section II on why to defect in Single-Shot PD is that it is better to play D whether partner plays C or D, so there really is no point in attempting to determine what partner will play. That is, however, not correct. The case for playing D when the partner is known to be playing D is incontrovertible. The case for playing D when partner is known to be playing C is, however, questionable. It is only when we realize that knowing what partner will play is important that we will make an effort to obtain that information, and it is only when we realize that this information can be obtained that we will seriously study what to do if partner is known to be playing C. Hence, let us break the impasse and assume that partner is known to be playing C.

What should you play when you know that partner will play C? You should play C, not D, because C is a sustainable strategy, while D is not. A population all pledged to play C when partner plays C can sustain cooperation, and achieve the reward payoff resulting from cooperation. However, attempts to obtain the temptation payoff by playing D against partners known to be playing C cannot succeed in the long run. Players attempting this strategy will soon find that no partner will cooperate with them, and they will receive the punishment payoff. In other words, one should be satisfied to accept the reward payoff when it is offered; it is not wise to use a strategy for temporary gain when it results in long-term loss. More than unwise, defecting when partner has committed to cooperation is a form of cheating, a violation of an implied trust that cooperation will be reciprocated.

The need to reject illusory immediate gain for the sake of sustainability is not unique to the Prisoner's Dilemma. Perhaps the closest analogy is a chain-letter scheme, where you receive a letter asking you to pay the sender an amount of money, say $100, and then send copies of the letter to a number of other people, say two others, who will duplicate the process and each send you $100. You stand to make a profit of $100, and so will everyone else who can enlist two more participants. Nevertheless, you should reject participating, and the simplest reason is that the process is not sustainable; it is just not possible for everyone in a population to achieve a gain without making a contribution. Another example of an unsustainable strategy is an attempt by government to overcome a shortfall in national income by printing additional money. We know the failure mode of that attempt — inflation. A last example comes from control system engineering. The performance of a device, for example a power amplifier, can be improved by comparing the actual output with the desired output, inverting and amplifying the difference, and feeding this signal back into the device. The greater the amplification, the smaller the difference signal driving the process, and hence the closer the actual output to the desired output. Because of response delays and other considerations, there is a limit on how fine a response we can obtain from a device. Excessive amplification in an attempt to obtain more than the system can deliver is defeated in this case also — here by spontaneous oscillations (singing) of the system.

It is encouraging to report that the performance of typical human subjects in Single-Shot PD experiments is much closer to the strategy advocated here than to the "defect" recommendation of most analysts. In an experiment reported by Cornell University economics professor Robert H. Frank,[7] 89 students (68 percent) cooperated and only 39 defected. Furthermore, 83 percent of subjects who predicted that their partner would cooperate cooperated themselves, while 85 percent of those who predicted defection by their partner defected themselves. The subjects formed those impressions during a 30-minute meeting with prospective partners prior to the game, but their play was kept confidential by the experimenter, who added a random amount of money to the PD game payoffs to prevent players deducing partner's play from the payoff received.

Single-Shot PD Strategy

Realization that it is proper to play C when partner is known to be playing C can be translated into the following strategy: commit to playing C with any partner who will similarly commit to play C with any partner so committed. Such players will be termed cooperators. Players who play D instead of observing this protocol will be termed defectors. The strategy of cooperators additionally is to play D with partners who are known defectors.

Consider now the following model: There exists a large population of cooperators and defectors. Members of this population meet one another randomly to play Single-Shot PD, each member having many such encounters over time. All past play is common knowledge. Defectors play D with all partners. Cooperators play C with each other, but recognize defectors (at least after they have played once) and play D against them.

It is obvious that cooperators will fare better than defectors in the above situation. Defectors will receive the P (punishment) payment from all encounters, while cooperators will receive the same P payoff in encounters with defectors, but will receive the higher R (reward) payoff in encounters with other cooperators. Note that the model postulates that an individual has many Single-Shot PD encounters over a lifetime, but not necessarily ever more than one with the same partner. This is a reasonable model of human Single-Shot PD encounters. A model that specified, on the contrary, that a person would encounter a PD situation only once in a lifetime would be unrealistic, and hence not a worthy model in which to invest major attention. Another assumption of the above model, namely that a PD partner's character, or history of PD play, can always be correctly assessed, is however not realistic. Whereas the cooperators need to distinguish cooperators and defectors, it is to the advantage of defectors to masquerade as cooperators. It will hence be assumed that the system set up by cooperators to identify defectors will be only partially successful. The following model shows that the cooperators will prevail even when assessment of partner's character, or history of PD play, is imperfect, provided such assessment is sufficiently good.

Assume a large population of cooperators and defectors. Let the fraction of cooperators be c. Members of the population meet randomly to play Single-Shot PD. Defectors Play D against everybody. Cooperators always correctly identify each other, but identify defectors only with probability y (because defectors attempt to masquerade as cooperators). Cooperators play D with partners identified as defectors, and play C with all others.

The expected payoffs are then as follows, using the payoffs from Figure 5-2, but setting $S = 0$, since this can be done without loss of generality:

The probability of a cooperator playing a cooperator is c, with payoff R, hence expected payoff cR.

The probability of a cooperator playing a defector is $(1-c)$, and the probability of playing and correctly identifying a defector is $(1-c)y$, with payoff P, hence expected payoff $(1-c)yP$.

The payoff for a cooperator playing a non-identified defector is 0.

Hence, the total expected payoff for a cooperator is

$$cR + (1-c)yP$$

The probability of a defector playing a defector is $(1-c)$, with payoff P, hence expected payoff $(1-c)P$.

The probability of a defector playing a cooperator who correctly identifies the defector is cy, with payoff P, hence expected payoff cyP.

The probability of a defector playing a cooperator who does not identify the defector is $c(1-y)$, with payoff T, hence expected payoff $c(1-y)T$.

Hence, the total expected payoff for a defector is

$$(1-c)P + cyP + c(1-y)T$$

Equating the total expected payoff for the cooperator with that for the defector, and solving for y, gives

$$y = [P + (T{-}P{-}R)c]/[P + (T - 2P)c]$$

For the payoff values of Figure 5-1, namely $P = 1$, $R = 3$, $T = 5$, this becomes

$$y = (1+c)/(1+3c) \qquad\qquad (5\text{-}1)$$

Whenever the value of y, the probability of correctly identifying defectors, is greater than the function above, the cooperators will do better than the defectors. The greater the fraction c of cooperators in the population, the less the value of y that is required for the cooperators to do better than the defectors. If, for an initial value of c, y is sufficiently high to give the cooperators the greater payoff, then it would be in the self-interest of defectors to convert and become cooperators. Since defectors are presumably motivated by short-term self-interest, they would presumably convert under those conditions.

For example, if half the population are initially cooperators, $c = 0.5$. Entering this in equation 5-1 yields $y = 0.6$, hence in this case a probability above 60 percent of correctly identifying defectors should persuade all defectors to convert to cooperation. Having done so, c is now 1, the corresponding value of y from equation 5-1 is now 0.5, and hence an identification probability above only 50 percent is now required to keep potential defectors from converting back to defection.

Note that the above is a plausible model of society. The mechanism that allows such a society to function is reputation. A reputation for honest dealing (cooperating when your partner cooperates) is a valuable commodity, and most members will not risk it for transient advantages. Members of society will cooperate to try to distinguish honest people from cheaters (defectors). It is to the benefit of everybody, cheaters included, to have as many honest members of society as possible; if there are too few of them, society as we know it breaks down.

Generalized PD Strategy

The previous strategy was designed for a population containing only cooperators and pure (all D) defectors. A general strategy must cope with any strategy employed by any other player, which might include selective rather than pure defection. Furthermore, a generalized PD game need not be limited to random Single-Shot PD encounters, but could include complex patterns of Single-Shot and varied-length iterated encounters of varying likelihoods, which could mimic the mix of encounters found in real society. A general TIT-FOR-TAT-like strategy is now proposed, which in the special cases of long Iterated PD and Single-Shot PD reduces respectively to the strategy TIT FOR TAT and to the Single-Shot PD strategy described in the previous subsection. The new strategy will be referred to as TIT FOR ETAT (from TIT FOR Extended TAT). The TIT FOR ETAT strategy is to respond with D if partner's last previous play with a cooperative partner was D, but otherwise to play C.

It will be assumed that all past play among the entire population is maintained as a public record. Furthermore, to eliminate the need for each player to delve indefinitely far back into the record in order to determine if a D played by a player was a defection justifying a D TIT by the next partner, or whether it was itself a justified D TIT hence requiring examining that player's previous play, the public record will indicate a current status for each player. The current status for any player will be C if the player's last play in the community was C. The current status for any player will be D if the last play was D with a partner whose current status was C. A play of D with a partner whose current status was D leaves the former player's current status unchanged. First-time players, or players whose status cannot be determined for any other reason, receive a current status of C. The TIT FOR ETAT rule then is to play whatever partner's current status is.

Note that the comments in Section III regarding TIT FOR TAT apply generally also to TIT FOR ETAT. Niceness is preserved by giving a player a current status of C (requiring a C response) unless defection for that player has been established. As with TIT FOR TAT, this risk of a one-time S payoff needs to be taken for the sake of establishing long-term cooperation. TIT FOR ETAT, like TIT FOR TAT, is forgiving; a single C play gets any player back into the good graces of the community. TIT FOR ETAT is provocable, unjustified defection provoking the TIT FOR ETAT community rather than TIT FOR TAT partner. The TIT FOR ETAT scheme is also quite clear.

Finally, TIT FOR TAT was only claimed to be a good, robust scheme, which might be improved upon in some situations. TIT FOR ETAT should be a similarly good, robust scheme. Since it lives in a more complex environment, it appears to be refinable in even more ways. To close this chapter, one possible refinement that might make TIT FOR ETAT more realistic, relating to vendettas, will be outlined.

A vendetta occurs when a player (X) who cooperates under most circumstances, for some reason selectively defects against one player (Y) repeatedly. A necessary response by Y is to play D with X. If X arranges always to play C with another player immediately before defecting against Y, then Y's play of D with X would earn Y defector status, making Y subject to being defected against in a subsequent play with TIT FOR ETAT players. The refinement in TIT FOR ETAT to overcome this possibility is to not downgrade the current status of a vendettee for playing D against the vendettor. What constitutes a vendetta would have to be carefully defined.

6

DOLLAR AUCTION

Dollar Auction is another non-zero-sum game in which the players often fare poorly. The rules of the game, and conventional ways in which it is played (poorly), are described in Section I of this chapter. A proposed cooperative scheme for playing the game (well) is presented in Section II. A variation of the game, in which the players have limited bankrolls, is described in Section III, because for this variation, a strategy has been proposed (O'Neill 1986) that is claimed to avoid the poor results of conventional strategies in the unlimited bankroll version of Dollar Auction. Pitting the O'Neill strategy against the author's strategy permits an examination of the treatment of conflicting strategies.

I. RULES AND CONVENTIONAL OUTCOMES

Dollar Auction differs from a conventional auction in two ways: (1) the object to be auctioned is a dollar (or more generally any fixed sum of money) rather than an object of uncertain value and (2) while the highest bidder receives the dollar in return for the high bid, the next-to-highest bidder (if any) must give the auctioneer the amount of the next-to-highest bid, but receives nothing in return. For example, if the first to last bids were respectively 5¢, 20¢, 25¢, 30¢, then the 30¢ bidder would receive $1 in exchange for the 30¢, while the 25¢ bidder would lose 25¢. In the basic Dollar Auction, the initial bid must be 5¢ or an integral multiple thereof, and each successive bid must exceed the previous bid by 5¢ or an integral multiple thereof.

When the Dollar Auction game has been played, often with a teacher as auctioneer and students as bidders, the bids have frequently exceeded $1, where *both* the high bidder and the next-high bidder lose; sometimes, the bidding has gone far above $1 (Raiffa 1982: 85–90, in which the Dollar Auction is called the Escalation Game). The reason for this is that the second-high bidder (X), who would stand to lose if the bidding ended, bids again in the hope that the previously high bidder (Y) will now give in; but this now makes Y the second-high bidder with a similar incentive to bid again. Even when the bidding goes beyond $1, the incentive is to reduce the loss by at least capturing the dollar (and perhaps to do better than the other bidder, although this is *not* supposed to be part of the objective). However, it is not only the naive that escalate; in discussing the playing of this game as an exercise in his graduate business course, Raiffa (1982) suggests that, at least in some phases of this exercise, a good strategy would be to plan to bid to some point beyond $1 if necessary, so as to capture the dollar from timid bidders.

II. CMS (COOPERATION WITH MINIMUM SANCTIONS) STRATEGY

The best result for the bidders is that one of them makes an initial bid of 5¢, and that no subsequent bid is made, the initial bidder thereby gaining 95¢. Cooperators should be able to manage this result as follows:

A determination is first required as to who gets to make the first bid. Since the rules of Dollar Auction, as of any auction, do not allow explicit communication among the bidders, a way must be found to give all bidders an equal chance to make the first bid. The obvious way to achieve this is to let the bidders compete freely in making the first bid (jump up alertly, or whatever making the first bid entails). The magnitude of the first bid is up to the first bidder, but there is nothing to be gained by making that bid anything other than 5¢. (If the auctioneer accepts as first bid the highest bid made in a time interval, this would revert the contest to conventional auction.)

Second, all cooperators, realizing that making a further bid is detrimental to the bidders as a group, refrain from making a further bid.

Third, any non-cooperator must be deterred from making a second bid, by making such an action unprofitable. This is a commitment that cooperators must firmly make, even though it may risk loss in a particular play of the game, in order to sustain the long-term gain from cooperation. The first bidder[1] must do the deterring, by being prepared to make over any second bid, a third bid with sufficiently high probability to make the second bid unprofitable. The process may have to be iterated. Thus, if the probability and magnitude of the third bid was such as to give a negative (or non-positive) expected value to the second bidder only in the absence of a fourth bid, then a fourth bid must be similarly deterred via the probability of a fifth bid, and so on.

An example will make this clear. First bidder makes a bid of 5¢, second bidder makes a bid of 10¢, and first bidder a bid of 15¢ with probability p. If there are no further bids, then the second bidder would gain 90¢ if the third bid were not made, and lose 10¢ if the third bid were made, for an expectation of $90(1-p) - 10p$ cents. To ensure that second bidder does not gain, p must be equal to or greater than 0.9. Relative to the 10¢ loss if the bidding ends at 15¢, second bidder can gain 90¢ by making a final bid of 20¢, but would lose another 10¢ if first bidder again raised the bid. The same relation holds for any three successive bids of x, $x+5$¢, and $x+10$¢. Hence, first bidder's strategy can be as follows: Whenever second bidder raises the bid by 5¢, first bidder raises the bidding a further 5¢ with probability p, and passes with probability $1-p$, where p is equal to or greater than 0.9. The strategy of the first bidder makes it unprofitable to enter the bidding after the first bid. Against an opponent who keeps escalating indefinitely, the expected loss to first bidder would be $5 + 10p + 10p^2 + 10p^3 + \ldots = 5 + 10p/(1-p)$ cents, which equals 95¢ for $p = 0.9$, thereby limiting the loss against the most recalcitrant opponent (who would be wiped out playing against another opponent using the same strategy).

Against an opponent who raises by the minimum increment (5¢), minimum increment raises (at the appropriate probability) to provide the deterrence appears to be the best course, since this provides the opportunity at the lowest level for the opponent to drop out. A situation where bidding increments are larger is described in the following section.

It is now suggested that the expected loss to the potential defector be made just sufficient to deter the defection, but no more than necessary. In the example, a probability p just in excess of 0.9 should suffice. Although the purpose of deterrence is that it should not have to be carried out, it is still well to keep the cost as low as possible, just in case it does have to be applied. Thus, for example, the probability p in the above example should be not much greater than 0.9, because the lower p, the smaller the cost if deterrence does have to be used. The proposed strategy for Dollar Auction is hence referred to as CMS (Cooperation with Minimum Sanctions). The approach will be generalized to apply to all non-zero-sum situations in Chapter 11.

The Dollar Auction has been invented as a non-zero-sum game played by the bidders, initially showing how the bidders play such a game badly by escalating the bidding, and showing in this section how the bidders can play the game well by cooperating. The auctioneer is in this scenario assumed to represent malevolent nature, over which no tears need to be shed.

It should be understood that such an approach should not be attempted in a legitimate auction, because collusion, even implicit collusion, by bidders in this event could ruin the auction as a useful societal mechanism, and would in many instances be illegal. In the legitimate auction, the bidders and the auctioneer are all participants, and the non-zero-sum payoff should include all of these parties.

III. DOLLAR AUCTION WITH LIMITED BANKROLL

In Dollar Auction with limited bankroll, a variation presented by Barry O'Neill (1986), each bidder can bid only to the limit of that player's bankroll. We will consider here the case where there are just two bidders, they have equal bankrolls of amount b, and both players know this.

To illustrate the kind of considerations involved, take the case where bankroll b is $1.55. Assume a bidder (1) has bid 60¢, with or without a previous bid. The other bidder (2) now cannot profit by making a bid. Bidder 2 cannot profit by bidding $1.55, because even if bidder 2 had previously made a bid as high as 55¢, the return from a $1.55 bid (a loss of 55¢) would not be greater than that from passing (a loss of any previous bid). However, for any bid less than $1.55, bidder 1 would respond by bidding untoppable $1.55, because that would represent a lesser loss for bidder 1 than paying 60¢ and not getting the dollar. Hence it would be foolish for bidder 2 to make a bid of less than $1.55, since (s)he would lose the amount of that bid. The 60¢ bid thus becomes a dominant bid.

The dominant bid is 95¢ below the bankroll, and this is true for any bankroll. Thus, if the bankroll is instead $2.50, $1.55 would be a dominant bid. It would not pay any bidder to contest this bid. The dominance gets reflected downward. Since a $1.55 bid would not be contested, $1.55 has the same practical effect as a $1.55 bankroll limit. Since a $1.55 bankroll causes 60¢ to be a dominant bid, a $2.50 bankroll should do so as well. This can be stated more compactly as that ($2.50)mod(95¢) is a dominant bid. The expression (b)mod(y), short for (b)modulo(y), merely means that as large an integral multiple of y is to be subtracted from b as possible without the result becoming negative.

Based on such reasoning, O'Neill has proposed the following strategy, hereafter referred to as BON, for the Dollar Auction with bankroll limit b:

Rule 1: Player 1, the player with the first opportunity to bid, should be $5¢ + (b–5¢)\mod(95¢)$.

Rule 1a: Player 2 should pass when player 1 makes an opening bid according to Rule 1.

Rule 2: With current bids of x_i and x_j, $x_j > x_i$, player i (the x_i bidder) should bid $x_j + 5¢ + (b-x_j-5¢)\mod(95¢)$ if this bid is less than $x_i + \$1$, and pass otherwise.

For example, for $b = \$2.50$, player 1 should bid 60¢ (Rule 1). If player 2 then made a bid of less than $1.55 (instead of passing as recommended by Rule 1a), player 1 should bid $1.55 (Rule 2). If player 2 then made a further bid of less than $2.50 (in violation of Rule 2), player 1 should bid $2.50 (Rule 2), the maximum allowable, thereby ending the game.

The BON strategy has the desirable properties that: if both bidders observe it, there is no escalation, and the bidder making the bid makes a profit; and no player violating the BON strategy can make a profit when playing with a player who observes it. BON also has some serious drawbacks. It fails to obtain the optimum 95¢ profit for the first bidder (except when $(b–5¢)(\mod 95¢)$ happens to equal 0). The bidding escalates rapidly when a BON player is paired with a non-BON player, for example, one who will raise by 5¢ a few times. Finally, Rule 2 is based on the assumption that the other player will observe the BON strategy, whereas two players both observing the BON strategy could never get to a situation that Rule 2 covers.

Reconciling CMS and BON

The CMS Strategy applies to Dollar Auction with a bankroll limit as well as to unlimited Dollar Auction, as long as bankroll b is at least \$1. (For b less than \$1, a bid of b cannot be deterred, hence bidding b immediately is the only viable strategy). Therefore, both CMS and BON are applicable to Dollar Auction with a bankroll limit (of not less than \$1). When only two CMS bidders participate, each player gains 47-1/2¢ per auction on the average. When only two BON bidders participate, each player gains 20¢ on the average when b = \$2.50 (the gain varies from 2-1/2¢ to 47-1/2¢ for other values of b). When a BON bidder and a CMS bidder participate, the following occurs, for b = \$2.50: When BON bids first, the bid is 60¢, and CMS passes. When CMS bids first, the CMS bid is 5¢, to which BON responds with a bid of 60¢ by Rule 2. If CMS recognizes that to be BON strategy, which the 60¢ bid strongly suggests, CMS would make the ultimately least costly response, namely a bid of \$1.55, with probability (p) sufficiently high to make the 60¢ bid unprofitable. The expected value of the BON bid is $(1-p)40¢ - (p)60¢$; the value of p making this zero is p = 0.4, so that a probability somewhat greater than 0.4 should be selected. The loss by CMS if CMS did not respond to the 60¢ bid would be 5¢; with a 0.4 probability of bidding \$1.55, the expected loss by CMS is $0.4(5¢) + 0.6(55¢)$, which is 35¢.

The encounter between CMS and BON is not untypical of real-life encounters. Each is acting on a principle which the player believes to be right, and thereby doing worse than each would do if they could reach agreement. How might they reach agreement?

Now that BON has become aware of the CMS strategy, BON might consider that CMS is better and convert. Or an arbitrator might be engaged, and come to that decision. It is certainly true that if everyone played CMS, everyone would fare better than with everyone playing BON, or with a mixture of CMS and BON players.

Another type of agreement is, however, possible. BON might be uncomfortable with the CMS obligation to deter, and believe the $5¢ + (b-5¢)\mod(95¢)$ initial bid to be least risky against other than CMS players. There is, however, no conflict between CMS and the BON initial bid. The only thing that needs to be fixed is the BON response to an initial bid of $5¢$. BON Rule 2 assumes any $5¢$ initial bid to be made by a BON player who made an inexplicable error, but will thereafter play party-line BON. In a world in which CMS is prominent, that is clearly an untenable assumption. If BON will grant that the $5¢$ bid was likely made by a CMS player, or another non-BON player, then the justification for Rule 2 disappears. If BON amends Rule 2 to pass a $5¢$ initial bid, then all interference between BON and CMS disappears, and both will be better off for it. The relative merits of CMS and the amended BON strategy could then be determined by their performance in various possible environments of Dollar Auction competition. (Can communism and capitalism resolve their differences in an analogous manner?)

7

COMPLEX GAMES

The objective in studying games like Prisoner's Dilemma and Dollar Auction is to isolate basic elements of conflict situations and thereby learn to understand these elements. Real human conflicts are, however, vastly more complex. Having learned what we can from the elemental games, we should go on to the study of more complex games, which might provide further insight on how to deal with human conflict. Obvious expansions of a game like Prisoner's Dilemma, such as by adding noise, more than two choices of moves, and asymmetric payoffs, do not go very far toward capturing the subtleties of human conflict, and may hence miss phenomena that are important in the solution of human conflict. We have, however, developed games that fully engage human capabilities, namely the games that humans commonly play.

The games that humans commonly play are, however, overwhelmingly zero-sum games. This is unfortunate. The games we play are such an important part of our lives. In addition to giving us pleasure, they are presumed to help prepare us for real life. Football is said to ready its players for the rough and tumble of business, and chess is encouraged in war colleges to sharpen strategy skills useful in battle. Since real-life conflicts are, however, generally non-zero-sum, the lessons learned from zero-sum games may be inappropriate in dealing with our personal, national, and international problems. What we need are non-zero-sum games of complexity comparable to those that people avidly play, both to provide that experience for the general population and as a vehicle for non-zero-sum-game research. If such games became popular, the strategies that successful players then evolved might give insight into how to best play complex non-zero-sum games, which in turn might be useful in resolving real-world problems such as international disputes.

With this motivation, I have devoted some effort to devising non-zero-sum games that people might find interesting to play. Perhaps the most expeditious way of introducing such games is to convert well-known zero-sum games into non-zero-sum versions. Three games that lend themselves well to such conversion are Scrabble, bridge, and basketball, and their non-zero-sum versions are presented in Chapters 8–10. The conversions are accomplished by changing the scoring of each of the games so that the objective of each player becomes the maximization of that player's individual score, rather than the zero-sum objective of scoring more than the opponent, in the conventional versions of the games. It turns out that in these three games, such a change can be made while leaving intact their essential character and the skills needed to play the games.

The important new element, when zero-sum games are converted to non-zero-sum games, is that players can now gain by using cooperative strategies. It is important to distinguish, however, between the volitional non-zero-sum cooperation that now becomes a consideration, and the cooperation that is required in conventional team games. In a conventional team game, such as basketball, a team's score belongs to the entire team, not to any individual player. Complete cooperation of the members of the team is expected in a single-minded objective of defeating an opposing team. In the non-zero-sum version of basketball to be presented in Chapter 10, this cooperation is made optional, with individual players becoming the beneficial owners of the basket points they score. The non-zero-sum game (within a game of opposing another basketball team) that a member of a team must now play is to get a fair share (or more) of the opportunities to score points while cooperating to enhance scoring in the face of the other team's opposition.

While well-known games are almost all zero-sum, and none have the non-zero-sum characteristics of the games to be described in Chapters 8–10, some deviations from strictly zero-sum games should be noted. Some games, such as golf and bowling, are comparative-performance-against-nature games. Whether they are zero-sum games depends on whether the primary goal is to beat other players, or to put on a good performance regardless what the other players do; but in either case, the capability of one player to influence the score of another is rather limited. Racing (particularly of runners) does offer some opportunity for cooperation, if one of the objectives of the racers is to achieve a faster race, and if they cooperate to increase the speed of the race.

When the objective of all the players coincides, the competitive aspect disappears, and the activity is one of joint puzzle-solving rather than a game as here defined. Such activities are sometimes referred to as noncompetitive or cooperative games[1]; they do not address how to resolve conflict situations. Note that zero-sum games (in which opponents have no commonality of interest) and noncompetitive games (in which all players have complete commonality of interest) are at opposite extremes of the game spectrum, with non-zero-sum games in between.

8

NON-ZERO-SUM SCRABBLE

Scrabble crossword game[1] is a game for two to four players (most often two in tournament play) in which the players take turns for the opportunity to place letter tiles on a special board to form words, thereby obtaining a score which depends, among other things, on the letters of the new words formed by the play (each letter of the alphabet has a specific point value) and the position of these letters on the board. (See Note 2 for a further description of the game.) The important game characteristics, for our purpose, are that there is a skill-requiring task of forming high-scoring words, and that a particular play not only determines the immediate score accruing to that player, but can significantly influence the prospects of the other player (or players) on subsequent play. The objective in conventional Scrabble is to obtain a higher score than the other player(s) at the board, hence along with obtaining a high score for self, strategy consists of limiting the opportunities for the other player(s).

The conventional version of the game can be converted into a Non-Zero-Sum Scrabble crossword game, hereafter abbreviated NZS Scrabble, by changing the objective for each player to that of obtaining as high a score as possible *regardless of the score of the other player(s)*. The skill-requiring task of forming high-scoring words remains, but the strategy of limiting opportunities for the other player(s) is changed to one of inducing cooperation from partner(s) to make this a mutually high-scoring game. (The attainable combined score in NZS Scrabble depends greatly on the degree of cooperation.) There is still conflict; a choice spot on the board grabbed by one player makes that spot unavailable for a (possibly higher) score by a partner.

In developing a strategy for NZS Scrabble with two players, it is apparent that at least some aspects of the TIT FOR TAT strategy examined in Chapter 5 can be applied, but the situation is much more complicated. Instead of the binary choice cooperate or defect, a player has multiple choices of greater or lesser degrees of cooperation, and in response to perceived lack of cooperation, partner can employ various degrees of retaliation. However, the degree of cooperation or retaliation intended by one player may not be clear to the other; the second player (Y) cannot always fully evaluate the situation facing the first player (X) because the letter tiles available to X but not played are mostly unknown to Y. Further, failure by a player to make the most cooperative move available may be due to failure to find that move, rather than a deliberate attempt to take advantage of partner. Unlike the Prisoner's Dilemma, NZS Scrabble is asymmetrical at least to the extent that the players have different word-forming abilities;

hence the superior player, even when scrupulously following TIT FOR TAT, can achieve a (consistently) higher score than partner. Strategy near the end of the game, when retaliation in that game is no longer effective, poses an additional interesting question: will players continue to play nice through the end of the match with partner, merely to achieve a reputation that might help them in future play?

Retaliation for defection takes an interesting form when there are more than two players. If the move sequence for three players X, Y, and Z is $XYZX \ldots$, and Z does not cooperate sufficiently, then it is up to player Y to apply the sanctions, since this can primarily only be done by the player with the previous move. If player Y fails to do this, then player X should apply sanctions to Y.

Casual players of NZS Scrabble would undoubtedly learn techniques of cooperation from such a game. Furthermore, NZS Scrabble might be psychologically more satisfying than conventional Scrabble, since players can work on improving their game and being rewarded by increasing personal scores, rather than beating other players and being defeated by superior players. The word-forming skills and tactical skills are required to about the same degree in both versions; only the tactical objectives are different.

Knowledge about game strategies for complex non-zero-sum games will probably come about mostly through tournament play. In contrast to informal play, where there can be no objections to agreement among the players to modify the rules if they prefer to play that way, in serious tournaments that are intended to determine and reward the capabilities of the competing players and strategies, care must be taken that the non-zero-sum intent of the game is preserved. The tournament procedures suggested below are intended to present both zero-sum play when championship rivals meet in a game, and "cooperation" between partners exceeding that allowed by the rules.

In zero-sum games, players tend to enforce the rules of the game on each other. For example, in conventional Scrabble tournaments, players can challenge words formed by their opponents, and if a challenged word is not found in the official dictionary, it must be removed and the offending player loses that turn. (If a challenged word is correct, the challenger loses his/her turn.) In NZS Scrabble, players could "cooperate" by never challenging a word. There would then be nothing to prevent a player from presenting any letter-sequence as a word; such a game would hardly be Scrabble as we know it. Since electronic Scrabble-playing devices exist,[3] perhaps the best way of overcoming this and other possibilities of excessive "cooperation" is by computer-controlled monitoring. Such a monitor would permit use only of words in the computer-contained dictionary. Additionally, the monitoring system could manage tile selection (selecting tiles in the same pseudo-random sequences for parallel games in the tournament can reduce the influence of luck), keep score, enforce limits on time and number of turns per game (as otherwise there may be excessive cooperative jockeying to amass favored letter combinations), and maintain play-by-play records for future analysis.

At the other extreme, care must be taken that the tournament situation, in which the objective is to come in first, does not override the non-zero-sum character of the game. It would not do, for example, to decide the tournament winner by having two finalists meet in a head-to-head match, because such a match would of necessity be zero-sum. More generally, the results of a match between two players should never be used in determining the relative ranking of those players, because otherwise holding down partner's score might be rewarded, and the game would no longer be pure non-zero-sum.

A non-zero-sum tournament can be conducted by pairwise round-robin play, but scoring should not be simple summation for each player of the scores from all the matches.[4] Instead, relative scores of any two players (A and B) can be obtained from the matches each played with common partners (C, D, . . .). The winner might then be determined by an elimination procedure mimicking an elimination tournament (e.g., a draw of A vs. B, C vs. D, . . . with the winner from A, B vs. the winner from C, D), where the outcome of each stage of the elimination procedure is determined from the relative scores of the round-robin tournament.

9

NON-ZERO-SUM BRIDGE

One of the most popular card games, and certainly the one that is most highly organized and has an extensive literature, is contract bridge.[1] To popularize non-zero-sum games, it is hence very desirable to have a non-zero-sum version of bridge, which I propose below following a paragraph briefly introducing standard contract bridge.

Conventional contract bridge is a team game with two partners (e.g., North-South) playing against two opposing partners (East-West). The objective of the game for each side is to maximize the point score relative to the other side, hence making this a zero-sum game. A game of bridge consists of two phases, a bidding phase followed by a card-playing phase. The objective for each side in the card-playing phase is to take as many as possible of the thirteen contested tricks. The bidding phase determines which side gets to become the declarer, by making the higher bid, meaning that this side will receive a positive score from the card play if it takes at least the number of tricks specified by the contract, and a negative (relative) score otherwise. Also determined by the bid is the trump suit, the transformation from tricks taken to points scored (higher bids, if fulfilled, generally result in more points for a given number of tricks), and who on the declaring side plays the partnership's two hands (the other partner being "dummy"). An interesting aspect of bridge is the communication between partners, who need to describe their hands to each other (e.g., by the bids they make) in order to optimize the contract and the card play.

One approach to making bridge a non-zero-sum game, which I considered and abandoned, is making the goal for each partnership to score as many points as possible, regardless of the score made by the other partnership, similar to the case of non-zero-sum Scrabble. However, what this would lead to in bridge would be for the two partnerships to take turns at bidding redoubled grand slams (contracts to take all the tricks), and trying to lose all the tricks, which would result, for the other side, in the highest score possible in bridge. (Both sides should as preliminaries cooperatively arrange to reach that stage of the game where scores are highest, known as vulnerability, when the version of bridge played allows this.) Managing the card play to accomplish this, managing the bidding so that the side capable of losing all tricks gets the bid, and fairly and cooperatively balancing the scoring opportunities might require some game-playing skills. However, even if an interesting game could evolve from this, it would not be anything like the present game of bridge.

Instead of the relationships between the opposing partnerships, there is another relationship that can be modified in bridge, namely that between the partners. The partnership relation can be reduced from that of a team, owning the team score, to that of cooperative players, who benefit from cooperation with each other but who have their individual scoring objectives. This can be done by leaving all the bridge rules intact and adding the one following rule: The normal partnership score credited at the end of play of any deal of bridge shall be allocated between the partners in proportion to the tricks taken by their respective hands. For example, if North-South bid and make four spades for a score of 620 (120 trick points plus 500 rubber-bonus points), with 3 tricks taken by the North hand and 7 tricks taken by the South hand, then North scores 620x3/10 = 186 points and South scores 620x7/10 = 434 points. (A handy calculator at the bridge table is suggested.) The proposed bridge variation will hereafter be referred to as NZS (non-zero-sum) bridge, and the standard game will be referred to as ZS bridge.

NZS bridge hence is composed of two component games. One is the zero-sum game that the two partnerships play against each other. The zero-sum score is to be made explicit at the end of play between players by subtracting from each player's score the average of all players' scores. The other game component is the non-zero-sum game between the players of each partnership, where they cooperate to receive as high a score as possible relative to the other partnership, but compete to individually take as large a fraction of their partnership's tricks as possible.

I suspect that good NZS bridge play consists of not selfishly doing anything that will risk lowering the partnership's score, thereby preserving most ZS bridge techniques. On the other hand, where it can be done with negligible risk, each individual player should try to take the tricks in his/her hand. However, it will not always be clear whether a certain strategy taking more tricks in one player's hand jeopardized the partnership's score or not, and an interesting part of NZS bridge will be the treatment of those cases. (It should, of course, be understood that an instance of success of a particular play in bridge does not necessarily indicate that that play was the correct one.)

It should be noted that the temptation to defect (make a selfish play that risks reducing the score of a partnership) differs depending on the situation in the game. Defenders attempting to defeat a high contract by just one trick would not care much which defender took the trick, since the main value in defeating the contract is preventing a high opponent score from which both defenders would suffer equally. The same defenders might be tempted to compete much more keenly when declarer's contract seems destined to go down and yield a lot of penalty points, since each trick then represents many points to the defender taking it. On the side that buys the contract, being declarer rather than dummy may be quite valuable, since declarer might be able to maneuver to take most of the tricks in his/her own hand; this prospect could influence the bidding.

Bridge tournaments are frequently conducted in the form of duplicate bridge, which minimizes the influence of luck resulting from the deal of the cards, and this form of bridge is particularly suitable for NZS bridge tournaments. In duplicate bridge, there are a number of playing tables set up (say T tables) with a set number of bridge hands (typically four) to be played at each table successively by all players in the tournament. The deals are stored in special containers called duplicate boards; the cards for each hand are kept separated during the play of each deal and are restored separated after play, so that successive players at each position of each table play identical hands.

In ZS duplicate bridge, the bridge partner pairs in the tournament are divided into two groups, N-S pairs and E-W pairs (T of each). Each N-S pair plays the N-S hands at each of the tables against a different E-W pair, and the E-W pairs similarly play each set of E-W hands once against a different N-S pair. The scores of all the N-S pairs, who all played the same hands, are compared against each other, and the highest scoring pair becomes the N-S winner. There is similarly an E-W winner. No comparison is made between the E-W winner and the N-S winner. (Usually, instead of using raw scores, the performance of each N-S or E-W pair for each set of duplicate hands is rated 1 (worst) to T (best), and it is these ratings that are summed to determine the winner.)

The NZS duplicate procedure is quite analogous. The players in the tournament are divided into N, E, S, and W players, who each plays each of the corresponding hands facing different sets of players. It is not necessary to have the same partner throughout the tournament. For example, Figure 9-1 shows how 20 players can play 5 rounds at 5 tables such that each player meets each player of each different group just once. The scores of all the N (North) players (in the example, five players: N_1, N_2, N_3, N_4, and N_5) are compared against each other, with the highest of those scores determining the winner in that group. The players in the E, S, and W groups similarly compete against each other. Note that the players competing against each other never meet in a game, thereby satisfying the NZS tournament requirement (described in Chapter 8) that the result of a match between two players should never be used in determining the relative ranking of those players.

A possible perversion of NZS team games, including NZS bridge and NZS basketball, which should be guarded against, is collusion across teams. If, for example, in a round of bridge, N, S, and E colluded against W, then W would surely receive a poor score, and N, S, and E might be able to maneuver to divide the resulting gain. Since such collusion would be obvious to all, it can be prevented by making it illegal, for all non-zero-sum games.

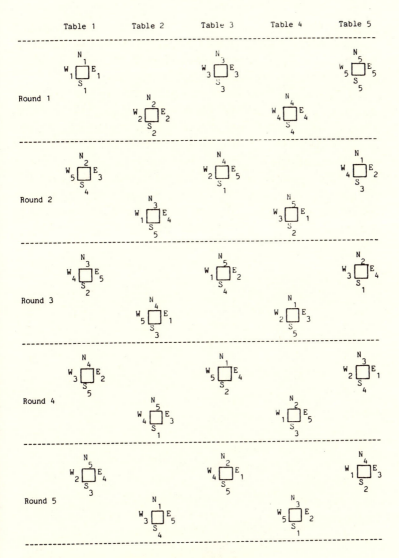

FIGURE 9-1 — Player Progression

To help understand the diagram, note for example that Player N_1 (one of 5 North players) progresses from table 1 in round 1, to table 5 in round 2, to table 4 in round 3, to table 3 in round 4, to table 2 in round 5.

10

NON-ZERO-SUM BASKETBALL

Zero-sum games that can be adapted to non-zero-sum play are not limited to purely intellectual games. Of the popular athletics games, the one that appears easiest to convert to non-zero-sum form is basketball, because all players have many opportunities to score, the scoring event can be unambiguously attributed to a specific player, cooperation is required to score well, and the distribution of the opportunity to score depends on the interaction among the players.

In basketball, the skill-requiring task is for each team to try to throw a ball through an elevated hoop, called a basket, against the opposition of the other team, while trying to prevent the other team from throwing the ball through its hoop. In conventional basketball, the objective of the game is for each team to attempt to obtain a higher score than the other team, accumulated through the award of one to three points (depending on the situation) each time the ball is thrown legally through the team's hoop.

Conventional basketball is converted to NZS (non-zero-sum) basketball by retaining the skill-requiring task and most of the present rules of the game, but changing the objective from team victory to the maximization of personal score of each player, where each player is to be indifferent to the score of other players. Such indifference could be supported by making player comparisons, rankings, and awards only with respect to games in the league for which the players to be compared did not appear in the same game (for the reason described in the "Tournament Procedures" section of Chapter 8). The score for each player is the conventional point value for each basket scored by that player, minus $(1/n)$ times the total basket points by the other team scored while that player is in the game, where n is the number of players per team playing simultaneously (five in a standard basketball game). The reason for the subtraction is to make the combined score of the teams zero; otherwise, it would be to the advantage of both teams to neglect defense and just run up the score, thereby losing much of the present integrity of the game. The non-zero-sum component of the proposed game is the interaction among the players of any team, who cooperate to increase the scores of each of them, but who are in competition for individual opportunities to score. It is obvious that team members who do not cooperate will fare poorly relative to those who cooperate well.

A way that members of an NZS basketball team might go about organizing themselves (likely with the help of coaches) is ,to establish norms of cooperative behavior: when players are entitled to take shots, when they should pass the ball but expect to get it back, when they should assist another player to score, and what their role is in defense. Equitable arrangements for shot-taking among players of differing abilities must be found. It is surely not wise to allow the weakest players to take extra shots so that all players on the team can have equal scores. On the other hand, players who are strong on defense (which benefits all team members) but weak shooters must be accommodated in some way, perhaps by the rest of the team arranging to get them the easy shots.

There might be defection from the above norm which might be overt or covert. Covert defection might be possible because the established cooperative behavior is difficult to define precisely, and small deviations might be hard to detect. Overt defection might occur because one or more players do not agree with the established norm, or because they do not subscribe to nice behavior. In any of those cases, the use of sanctions by the remaining players comes into consideration, followed by the reaction of the original defecting players, and so on. The five-person interaction of a normal-sized basketball team further makes the problem more complicated; however, NZS basketball teams of sizes down to two could be tried, possibly providing interesting comparisons (and still sufficient complexity).

The NZS variant of basketball has some additional advantages as a participant sport. In the conventional form of the game, coaches often have an overwhelming interest in having their team win, which sometimes conflicts with their acting in the best interest of each of their players. In NZS basketball, where team victory is not considered, coaches can concentrate their efforts on teaching and developing the players. Coaching and refereeing can be combined as league functions, and coaches might even be rotated among the teams so that all players can benefit from the diverse expertise of the staff. In addition to instructing the players and refereeing games, the coaching/refereeing staff could assign players equitably to teams and perhaps rearrange teams periodically, assure that all players get equitable playing time (no need for bench warmers in NZS basketball), and be available to mediate or arbitrate disagreements among members of a team. Team members, not coaches, would have the responsibility for making team decisions.

Although it would not be likely to replace the present form of basketball where teams represent such institutions as cities and schools, NZS basketball could even become a popular spectator sport; high-level golf, also solely concerned with the relative performance of its players, draws large on-site and television audiences.

A purpose of Chapters 7–10 has been to promote a new set of games whose adoption might benefit society. The games of Scrabble, bridge, and basketball appear particularly suitable for conversion to non-zero-sum games. I have described the thought process by which I arrived at the non-zero-sum versions of these games, with the hope that this will help game designers to come up with additional non-zero-sum games, perhaps including entirely novel ones without zero-sum counterparts. In addition to the societal benefits that NZS Scrabble, NZS bridge, NZS basketball, and further yet-to-be-invented NZS games might provide, they add a new dimension — the amount, implementation, and recognition of cooperation with other players — that could make games more interesting to play.

Popularized non-zero-sum games can provide a means for the better understanding of non-zero-sum situations. Controlled experiments are presently performed to better understand non-zero-sum behavior, but they are difficult, costly, and can involve only limited numbers of participants. On the other hand, with the widespread playing of non-zero-sum games, much information on non-zero-sum behavior may become available. Playing popular NZS games could be considered a diffuse alternative to concentrated experiments, in which many take part because the games are inherently enjoyable. All who desire can participate.

11

COOPERATION THE[ORY]

We have seen in previous chapters that cooperation pays in simple non-zero-sum games. Players
must be prepared to deter unfair moves by other
players, and care must be taken to avoid misunder-
standings between players. It was suggested that
we try playing more complicated non-zero-sum
games, such as non-zero-sum adaptations of
Scrabble, bridge, and basketball, to better understand how to use cooperation in those more
complicated situations. In this chapter, generalized
principles of cooperation are proposed, which are
consistent with the known successful strategies in
non-zero-sum games, and which are intended to
serve as standards of behavior in real-world situations where cooperation would be mutually beneficial
to all the parties involved (which includes almost
all real-world situations). These standards facilitate
the scheme for resolution of international disputes,

which will be described in the following chapter, Chapter 12.

In order for the participants in a non-zero-sum encounter to cooperate, which we know is necessary for them to achieve good results, there have to be some understandings between them of what each expects of the others, and toward what common goal cooperation should take them. In some games, such as Dollar Auction, the rules forbid communication between the players, and the understandings have to be implicit, based on prior general knowledge (in the future hopefully including the information in this book). In most real-world situations, however, communication is an important aid in planning and agreeing on cooperation.

The common goal toward which cooperation should take the participants may either be obvious in a particular non-zero-sum encounter, as in the Prisoner's Dilemma game, or may have to be worked out by the participants. It will be helpful to separate determination of the common goal, from the strategy that each participant in the encounter should use once the common goal is recognized. Accordingly, Section I of this chapter, "Standards of Cooperation," will show how cooperation in non-zero-sum encounters can be achieved once a common goal is recognized. This common goal is the selection, from the possible payoffs in the encounter, of those jointly sufficiently beneficial to all the participants. Section II of the chapter, "Welfare Satisfaction," describes how such a selection might be accomplished.

I. STANDARDS OF COOPERATION

Assume, then, that the participants in an ongoing relationship concur on the moves to be termed cooperative, namely those moves that, when taken by each, yield each a satisfactory payoff. Moves made contrary to this concurrence will be considered defection. A participant who defects might receive a larger payoff if everyone else continues to make the original cooperative moves, but the total payoff to all participants will be inferior (otherwise the altered move should have been included with those considered to yield satisfactory payoffs and hence considered cooperative). Similarly, multiple defections cause inferior payoffs. Note that the above is a generalization of, for example, the Prisoner's Dilemma game, in which the simplicity and symmetry of the game permitted the immediate naming of the moves "cooperation" and "defection."

Mere concurrence by a participant, say X, that a particular result will be mutually satisfactory, does not necessarily mean that X will cooperate to bring it about. If there were an action X could take that would yield X a greater payoff, thereby deviating from the mutually satisfactory result at the expense of the other participants, X might well try it, and the cooperation needed to bring about the mutually optimum result would not occur. In order to achieve cooperation, the proponents of cooperation must thus not only postulate the cooperative action to be taken by them, but must also react to defection in such a way that defectors will do worse than they would do if they cooperate. Proponents of cooperation can achieve their objectives, of making cooperation attractive to all parties, by establishing standards of behavior for cooperators respectively with each other, with known defectors, with participants of undetermined characteristics, and with participants of inferior strategy skills. A set of such standards is now proposed. The standards of cooperation are meant to apply to real-world situations as well as to more formal non-zero-sum games; to emphasize this, the terms "encounter," "participant," and "choose" will be used rather than the terms "game," "player," and "play," identified with game theory.

How to Cooperate with Fellow Cooperators

Cooperators hope that all participants in the non-zero-sum encounter will subscribe to being cooperators, and endeavor to provide a satisfactory payoff to all such subscribers. However, if any participant could unilaterally obtain a greater payoff than by making a cooperative choice, then that participant might well choose not to cooperate. Hence, the agreed-on cooperative payoff for any participant X must be no less than what X could obtain unilaterally, that is, with all subscribers to the standards of cooperation making the decisions most unfavorable to X. (For a refinement of this condition, see the subsection on coalitions in Section II). The mutually satisfactory payoff to be agreed on by the cooperators is hence constrained to give no participant less than what that participant could obtain unilaterally. All subscribers to this standard then agree to cooperate in encounters with fellow subscribers so as to bring about the agreed-on, mutually satisfactory payoff, and, as will be shown, it is to the advantage of all participants to observe the cooperative standards.

How Cooperators Should Deter Defectors

Defection is defined as a choice other than the cooperative standard, by a participant in a non-zero-sum encounter, for the purpose of increasing the payoff to that participant while degrading the non-zero-sum payoff to all the participants. If the defectors were successful in thus increasing their payoffs relative to cooperation, then there would be little incentive to keep cooperating; cooperation would collapse and its advantage to all participants would be lost. In order to keep this from happening, cooperators must deter defection by others by not allowing a participant to gain from a defection strategy. Such a gain must be prevented even if there is an additional cost to cooperators to implement prevention of gain by the defector.

The strategy chosen by cooperators to deter defection should be that which can be achieved at least cost, in case it has to be actually carried out. As long as defection is made unprofitable, there seems little to be gained by making it more unprofitable at higher cost. If making defection unprofitable turns out not to have deterred it, then the situation is not understood and must be re-evaluated, rather than blindly increasing the sanctions. It should be especially noted that it is neither necessary nor advisable to make the loss to the defector greater than the cost to the cooperator; such zero-sum mentality could lead to a nasty escalation of punitive measures. The reason for failure to achieve cooperation even in the face of an adequate deterrence strategy might be a disagreement or misunderstanding on a fair division of payoff, contrary to the assumption here made that there is concurrence on this. Resolving such a dispute is discussed in Section II, "Welfare Satisfaction"; it cannot be resolved by mutual sanctions each trying to defend a different division of payoff. In any case, the standard of minimum cost sanctions will limit the losses in such a situation.

Whether there is a cost attached to applying a sanction depends on the particular situation. For example, for the iterated Prisoner's Dilemma game, described in Chapter 5, the appropriate deterrence strategy is TIT FOR TAT. TIT FOR TAT causes sufficient loss to the defector to make each instance of defection unprofitable; a greater sanction would increase the risk that cooperation would not be resumed after a single instance of defection, while lesser sanction would allow some defection to be undeterred. (For example, a strategy of TIT FOR TWO TATS, one of the strategies entered in Axelrod's tournaments, would allow a defector to get away with a single defection.) There is no cost to applying the TIT FOR TAT sanction, since apart from the effect on the other player's play, the D play constituting the sanction yields its player the highest return on that move. On the other hand, it was shown that there can be a cost involved in applying a sanction in the Dollar Auction game, and that this cost can be minimized.

Where there are more than two participants in an encounter for which there is a cost to applying sanctions, there is a question of how responsibility for applying sanctions is to be divided. The fair allocation of the burden of applying sanctions is analogous to the fair divisions of the payoff in a non-zero-sum encounter, and cooperative standards for performance of this task should be developed. Failure to apply sanctions when required by the cooperative standards is a form of defection, and should be deterred in a similar manner. The deterrence sequence converges, since at each higher level of deterrence, there is one less participant still available to do the deterring. For example, in non-zero-sum Scrabble with more than two players at the board, sanctions on a defecting player Z must necessarily be implemented by the player Y whose turn precedes Z; and if Y neglects to apply required sanctions, then it is incumbent on player X whose turn precedes Y to apply sanctions to Y, and so on if there are more players.

Of course, the whole purpose of this system of deterrence standards is to safeguard the desired system of cooperation, and sanctions should not normally have to be applied.

How Cooperators Should Consider Unknowns as Cooperators

Cooperators should consider participants of unknown characteristics and unknown prior performance to be cooperators unless proven otherwise, and to act accordingly. This is a generalization of the strategy of playing nice, never being the first to defect, that was so essential in the Axelrod tournaments of the iterated Prisoner's Dilemma. This is a necessary risk that cooperators must take, for to choose otherwise would not allow cooperation to get started. It would, however, be wise to minimize the risk of poor payoff in early encounters by contending for small stakes initially with an unknown participant, when this is possible. Where there is probabilistic information about the unknown participant, such as in the noisy Prisoner's Dilemma game, then the details of the situation should determine how high the probability that the unknown participant has defected should be to treat that participant as a defector.

When and How Cooperators Should Protect Inept Participants

Whether cooperators should take advantage of inept participants, that is, participants who obtain less for themselves than they should when encountering cooperators, depends on the type of encounter. If the encounter is a game, especially a tournament game, where the score should reflect playing ability, then a superior cooperative player should, upon recognition, attempt to take maximum advantage of the inferior player.

In a real world of non-zero-sum encounters, however, a cooperator ought to be more compassionate, and not attempt to take advantage of a participant of inferior skill, particularly of inferior strategy skill. The cooperator is probably justified in attempting to obtain at least as large a payoff as would have been obtained with a skillful cooperative partner, but should probably not aim for more than that when so doing would degrade the overall non-zero-sum payoff.

The preceding four standards show how cooperators can prevail, providing they can concur on what choices are acceptable as cooperative choices. This in turn depends on concurrence on what are acceptable choices, or on the payoffs which result from those choices. Cooperators must thus establish a measure for the common welfare for all the participants in a non-zero-sum encounter. Staying within the range of choices which, when adhered to by all participants, makes that common welfare a maximum (or keeps it within an agreed-on margin of a presumed maximum), then constitutes cooperation.

II. WELFARE SATISFACTION

Cooperation in non-zero-sum encounters allows the participants to obtain larger payoffs than by working at cross-purposes. Successful cooperation requires that the Pareto optimal condition be satisfied, namely that all ways by which one participant could get more without another participant getting less have already been utilized, and that the payoff of one participant can be higher only in exchange for someone else's payoff being lower. Under those conditions, how should the payoff to each participant be determined?

Each participant might want a relatively large payoff for him/her/itself and a correspondingly small payoff for others, but this is not jointly possible. On the other hand, if each participant worked toward a different Pareto optimal outcome with a different set of payoffs, then the standards of cooperation previously determined might not be achieved, because one participant might consider as defection and apply a sanction to a choice another thought was cooperation, thereby causing a breakdown in cooperation. Success of cooperation requires agreement on what constitutes an acceptable set of payoffs, hence some principled way of determining which set of payoffs is in some sense mutually best for all participants. The measure of mutual desirability of payoffs to various participants is known as social welfare, or simply Welfare, W.[1] The cooperative participants must hence agree on how to determine Welfare W as a function of the payoffs to the individual participants, and define cooperation as only those choices leading to sufficiently high Welfare.

Welfare Function Alternatives

A possible welfare function is one where Welfare is the sum of the payoffs to the participants. This can be written symbolically as

$$W = \sum_{i=1}^{n} U_i \tag{11-1}$$

where U_i is the payoff to the ith participant, and the participants are indicated by subscript numbered i

through n, n being the number of participants. In a two-party encounter, equation 11-1 simplifies to

$$W = U_1 + U_2 \qquad (11\text{-}1a)$$

To illustrate the implications of this particular welfare function, suppose that two non-zero-sum Scrabble players can, if they cooperate, obtain either expected scores of 700 for player 1 and 200 for player 2, or of 500 for player 1 and 300 for player 2. (If they do not agree to cooperate for either of those sets of scores, player 1 obtains less than 500 and player 2 less than 200.) For welfare function 11-1a, Welfare from the 700,200 payoff, $W = 700 + 200 = 900$, is greater than that from the 500,300 payoff, $W = 500 + 300 = 800$, and the 700,200 payoff should hence be preferred. To appreciate the merits of this welfare function, assume that the players are entered in a tournament of multiple non-zero-sum games, including non-zero-sum bridge. Further assume that when they are partners in non-zero-sum bridge, players 1 and 2 have a similar choice of 200,700 or 300,500 payoffs, except here player 2 is the stronger player with the higher payoffs. (If they are serious competitors in the tournament, strengths in individual sports should balance out.) Cooperators who adopt the 700,200 payoffs would hence each have scores of 900, after a round of non-zero-sum Scrabble and non-zero-sum bridge, compared to 800 from corresponding rounds for competitors who adopt the 500,300 payoffs.

More generally, welfare functions of the type 11-1 which sum the payoffs to the individual participants are appropriate where there are many varying encounters of each participant with the members of a cooperative community, not necessarily multiple encounters with the same members. Maximizing the sum of the payoffs in each encounter will maximize the payoff to the community. If the types of encounters are sufficiently varied, then inequities that might in some sense exist in single encounters, such as the disparate 700,200 payoff in the Scrabble example, will tend to even out, and the higher overall payoff will be reflected in higher payoffs to each of the participants.

The payoff U_i is often expressed in units of utility, which was defined in Chapter 4, and constitutes the subjective value of the payment to the recipient, rather than a common objective value. It is utility that the recipient wishes to maximize. A problem with utility is the difficulty of its interpersonal comparability; different persons or entities might have different utility scales. To avoid consequent distortions, equations 11-1 and 11-1a can be rewritten as

$$W = \sum_{i=1}^{n} c_i U_i \qquad (11\text{-}2)$$

and

$$W = c_1 U_i + c_2 U_2 \qquad (11\text{-}2a)$$

where the c_i which multiply U_i are parameters that have to be agreed upon. Beside possibly different interpersonal utility scales, the parameters c_i also take care of other asymmetries in the participants; for example, when federations are formed, the question often arises whether prerogatives of entities should be weighted equally, or proportional to population, or in some intermediate fashion.

Many results in game theory are premised on the condition that interpersonal utility comparisons not be made.[2] This leads, for two participants, to welfare functions of the form

$$W = c_0(U_1-U_{10})(U_2-U_{20}) \qquad (11\text{-}3a)$$

which can be extended for n participants to

$$W = c_0 \prod_{i=1}^{n} (U_i-U_{i0}) \qquad (11\text{-}3)$$

where Welfare is proportional to the product of utilities U_i of the individual participant i relative to some reference utility U_{i0}. It is seen that W is independent of the relative scaling of the individual utilities; hence that scaling will not affect the payoff that causes W to be a maximum. (c_0 is a multiplier that merely makes the units of Welfare independent of those for utility.)

A major problem with welfare functions 11-3a and 11-3 is what to use for reference utilities U_{i0}. Game theorists often propose that U_{i0} be the smallest, or most negative, value that player i could suffer through manipulative strategies by other players. This makes it advantageous for all players to develop threat strategies to lower the reference utilities of other players, because the lower this reference, the bigger U_i-U_{i0} for a given value of U_i and hence proportionally less a given increase in U_i will increase W. This is disadvantageous to player i and consequently advantageous to other players, since preference is given to those payoffs that result in bigger Welfare increments.

Note that the threats resulting from the above approach to determining reference utilities are entirely different from the sanctions previously recommended for assuring cooperation. The lowering of reference utilities is not limited in any way; in fact, the lower the reference utility of an opponent, the better, according to this approach. The real-life analog of a low reference utility is war capability. With this approach, the relatively more damage in war one nation could wreak on another, the better the terms it ought to be able to negotiate between them. The approach encourages threats (which may be misunderstood and carried out). It does not appear to be a good cooperative solution to non-zero-sum problems.

It is therefore strongly recommended that the reference utilities U_{i0}, if welfare function 11-3a or 11-3 is to be utilized, be determined differently. The recommendation is that they be the lowest Pareto optimal value for each participant; in other words, threats to create a payoff to one participant that could be raised without lowering anyone else's payoff should be ignored. The recommended Pareto optimal reference utilities are superior to the threat utilities in every way that I have been able to determine. Recall that the purpose of the welfare function is to enable cooperators to define cooperation. Once cooperation is defined, then cooperators have the mechanism previously described to elicit cooperation from all participants. It is, hence, incongruous to define cooperation among cooperators on the basis of how much each could damage others in the absence of cooperation. That is precarious truce rather than cooperation.

As an illustration of welfare function 11-3a with the reference utilities U_{i0} of the lowest Pareto optimal values, as here recommended, consider the Scrabble example (ignoring for the moment that welfare function 11-3a may not be suitable for this example). Here U_{10}, the lowest Pareto optimal payoff to participant 1, is 500; and U_{20}, the lowest Pareto optimal payoff to participant 2, is 200. Welfare W from equation 11-3a for the 700,200 payoff is then $c_0(700-500)(200-200) = 0$, and for the 500,300 payoff is $c_0(500-500)(300-200)$ and is also zero. The participants can, however, do better than this, by randomly choosing the 700,200 or 500,300 payoff with equal probability (e.g., by flipping a coin on the first encounter, and alternating thereafter). Then the expected payoff would be 600,250, with corresponding $W = c_0(600-500)(250-200) = 5000c_0$. Although the 600,250 payoff maximizes welfare function 11-3a, it should be observed that it does not maximize the welfare function 11-1a. The value of W from equation 11-1a for the 600,250 payoff is $600 + 250 = 850$, compared to the value of 900 for the payoff 700,200.

Welfare functions 11-3a and 11-3 originated for the situation where utilities of participants are not intercomparable. However, it is also plausible for a single encounter not ever connected in any way to any other encounter, or for multiple encounters that are essentially repeats of such an encounter, with the participants always in the same relative position. In such cases, the participants are so little interconnected that they do not give credence to the utility comparability. This is at the other extreme from the condition of much varied interaction where welfare function 11-2 applies.

Where the situation is somewhere intermediate between the two cases just described, a welfare function which combines welfare function 11-2 and 11-3 might be utilized, such as

$$W = \sum_{i=1}^{n} c_i U_i + c_0 \prod_{i=1}^{n} (U_i - U_{i0}) \tag{11-4}$$

Choice of the c parameters permits adjusting welfare function 11-4 to become welfare function 11-2 or 11-3, or anywhere in between.

For two-party encounters, 11-4 simplifies to

$$W = c_1 U_1 + c_2 U_2 + c_0 (U_1 - U_{10})(U_2 - U_{20}) \tag{11-4a}$$

Much more complicated welfare functions than the simple ones described in this section might be selected in practice. However, what we need to consider next is how agreement on a welfare function can be reached when cooperative participants initially propose differing welfare functions.

Reaching Agreement on Welfare Function

How can cooperators devise a welfare function to which all are willing to subscribe? They should imagine themselves as each of the members of the community whose function is to be determined. In the important special case of a two-party encounter, they should imagine themselves in each of two positions, including all the subjective values held in that position. Each party should then propose the welfare function that it would prefer in ignorance of the position which it actually occupies.

The above is of course hard to do, because in most cases the participants are not ignorant of their position and find it difficult to put themselves in the other's position. One of the purposes of negotiation is to educate each other thoroughly about each other's situation. Determination of welfare functions is easiest when each differing situation can be made part of some higher overall principle. One advantage of using an arbitrator to resolve disputes on welfare function is that arbitrators might find it easier to imagine themselves in the positions of the various contending participants. Such an ability to understand and empathize with the various contending viewpoints is an important skill required of arbitrators.

Welfare function determination should be an honest search for a best welfare function. We will now presume such an honest search, deferring to a subsequent section the consideration of deception, where a participant knowingly attempts to distort the welfare function for the purpose of thereby gaining a larger payoff for that participant. Proposals by the various participants for a common welfare function will hence be considered to be best effort approximations, colored by different background, to an uncertain optimal welfare function.

The form in which welfare functions are expressed will, of course, depend on the negotiators, and it is not implied here that it is necessary, or even recommended, that they be in a mathematical form. However, no matter how difficult or impractical it is to quantify the consequences of textual agreements, the consequences of each clause in an agreement is surely valued in some way by each negotiator. The description here on reaching welfare function agreement, made in somewhat mathematical language, should not be misread as implying that negotiators need to be conversing in that form.

One way of resolving differences in the welfare function proposed by various participants is to find an expression including parameters, whose values can be adjusted to yield the various proposed welfare functions. This was illustrated in the previous section with the construction of equation 11-4. The parameters, such as the c coefficients in equation 11-4, can be considered as uncertainties in an otherwise agreed-on welfare function. The reason for the uncertainties is that our present knowledge in what yields the best social welfare is incomplete, and hence these uncertainties are to be resolved through some combination of research, negotiation, and arbitration.

Research is the ultimate means of attaining knowledge, including inquiry into welfare function parameters, which should lead to the reasons for the uncertainties in the parameter values and to reduction in the uncertainties. Some disputes, however, cannot wait for ultimate resolution by research; in that case, the differences should be resolved or at least narrowed by negotiation. At some stage of the proceedings, all agreed-on higher principles will have been utilized, and remaining differences are subjective, resulting from different experiences and makeup of the participants. Of course, the better the participants understand each other, the more successful they should be at narrowing differences. Even where differences cannot be resolved completely, it is advantageous to narrow them as much as possible by research and negotiations before going to the next step, arbitration.

At the point where arbitration is to be utilized, it will be the least-cost way to proceed. Such other alternatives as leaving the difference unresolved, or engaging in war or some other destructive dispute-resolution contest, will be less desirable to all the participants. Since the parties, as cooperators, only require that the arbitrator be competent and *unbiased* (to try to obtain an arbitrator who is biased toward your side would be considered dishonest), arbitrator selection should be relatively easy compared to negotiation of long-held remaining parameter value differences.

Once agreement has been reached on a welfare function, the maximum value that can be attained with the proper choices by the participants can be determined, and those choices would be designated as cooperative choices and required of cooperators. However, welfare satisfaction, which will now be described, might be a more practical goal. In welfare satisfaction, the acceptable Welfare is an agreed-on amount less than the maximum value of the agreed-on welfare function. Choices which permit this acceptable Welfare level to be reached will be considered to be cooperative. In other words, cooperators are permitted a controlled degree of competition, such that the degradation in Welfare due to this competition is within an agreed-on amount. When such competition is allowed, the participants might be able to agree on a simpler welfare function. The savings in the cost of welfare function determination might then exceed the Welfare loss due to the allowed competition.

It needs to be repeated that there is a constraint on the range of the welfare function where all of the above will work. The payoff to each participant, from the choices that are agreed-on as cooperative, must be no less than the payoff that that participant could obtain unilaterally when all cooperators are arrayed against that participant, since there is no way to compel a participant to accept a smaller than unilaterally obtainable payoff. Hence, in the welfare maximizing or welfare satisfying calculations, only that portion of the welfare function can be considered where each participant obtains at least as much as that participant could obtain unilaterally. Uncertainty must be resolved in favor of reducing usable welfare function range, because the cooperation scheme will not work if a participant thinks (honestly, even if incorrectly) that (s)he can obtain more unilaterally. In many applications, including those where the unilateral choice is war, it is obvious that the payoff any participant could obtain unilaterally is far worse than that obtained from Welfare satisfaction, and hence does not constrain the Welfare calculations.

Where there are only two parties interacting simultaneously (also known as a two-person non-zero-sum game), the above constraint suffices. Where there are more than two parties interacting simultaneously (also known as an n-person game), the possibility of coalitions introduces an additional complication. That topic is taken up next.

Downplaying of Coalitions

When there are more than two simultaneous participants in an encounter, coalitions can occur. Mathematicall n-person game theory (for $n > 2$) is largely concerned with coalition formation. The theory is nowhere near complete, but the sense I get of the theory is of a mad scramble among players to form coalitions to give those players maximum advantage over players outside their coalition, while players outside those coalitions attempt to prevent or break or join those coalitions by offering players in them favorable terms for the proposed alternatives. The players in the coalition are, of course, busy attempting to defend their coalitions or allowing themselves to be bribed into more advantageous ones, or taking on the methods of the outs if their coalition collapses.

The above process is at variance with what cooperators are trying to achieve, namely agreement for all participants to achieve a collective best result. Success by defecting participants in forming coalitions, so that they can obtain through the unilateral choices of the coalitions larger payoffs than those consistent with collective best, would of course lower the overall Welfare. The cooperators should react as follows:

1. Where a coalition firmly exists, the range of the welfare function must be limited so that the payoff to the coalition, from the moves that are agreed-on as cooperative, is no less than the payoff the coalition could obtain unilaterally, similar to the situation with

individual participants. Again, in many applications, including those where the unilateral coalition choice is war, it is obvious that the payoff that a coalition could obtain unilaterally is far worse than that obtained from Welfare satisfaction, hence will not constrain Welfare satisfaction.

2. Neither negotiators nor arbitrators should attempt to determine or take into account possible coalitions that could be formed to the advantage of its conspirators. (This, incidentally, frees negotiators and arbitrators from having to deal with the intricacies of n-person coalition theory.)

3. The cooperators should take measures to prevent coalitions from obtaining payoffs in excess of those from collective Welfare criteria, with a firm policy of penalizing coalition instigation and using the proceeds as a bounty to break such coalitions. The policy of cooperators, not to attempt to attain a payoff larger than the agreed-on welfare satisfying one, deters adverse coalitions. The following example illustrates this:

Consider a symmetrical game with three players, A, B, and C, where A and B are known defectors and C is a cooperator. The game is symmetrical with total payoff of 45 when the three players cooperate, hence a reasonable agreed-on cooperative payoff would be 15 each. Let the rules of the game also state, however, that any coalition of 2 players obtains a payoff of 42, with 0 to the third player. Under these conditions, A and B might very well attempt to form a coalition and agree to split the payoff. This strategy would be in accord with their inclination to get the most for themselves (21 instead of 15), regardless of overall consequences (ignoring that, if C were a similarly cutthroat player, each coalition would succeed only 2/3 of the time, hence get an average payoff of only 14).

How can C force the cooperative solution? By stating that if one of the other players, say A, makes an offer to form a coalition to the other, in this case B, then C will offer that other player (B) to enter into a coalition and allow that player a payoff of 27, with C retaining only 15 of the payoff of 42 to the coalition (consisting of B and C). B, being a defector, would surely jump coalitions in order to receive the 27 payoff rather than 21 from the AB coalition. Hence, A dare not initiate a proposal for a coalition, since A would wind up being left out and receiving 0. Any proposal by either A or B that can yield the proposer more than the cooperative payoff of 15 would meet the same fate. Hence, C can force the cooperative solution.

Note that the above process would not work if C were not a cooperator. Then, A could disrupt the BC coalition by offering C a better split than C is getting in the BC coalition. Anticipating that this could happen, B would probably not be enticed to leave the AB coalition. It is the trust the others would have that C would not break the BC coalition in order to obtain a higher payoff, that would persuade B to switch coalitions, and that would hence prevent A from proposing a coalition in the first place. (Needless to say, C would not make or accept an initial move to participate in a coalition, because that would reduce Welfare and be self-defeating in the long run.)

Dealing with Deception

Welfare function determination has so far been described as an honest search for the best welfare function. It is possible, however, that a participant *knowingly* provides misleading information to obtain a welfare function giving that participant a larger share of the payoff. The misinformation could relate to welfare function parameters, to the payoff that the participant claims to be able to obtain unilaterally, or to the screening for non-bias of potential arbitrators.

In game theory, this topic is treated under the heading of incentive compatibility. Any private information provided by a player is to be utilized only to the extent that falsification of the information would not result in a gain by the falsifier. The cost of such an incentive compatible mechanism is that the Welfare is generally less than could be obtained if the players could be relied on to tell the truth in the absence of such a mechanism.[3]

A somewhat different approach is suggested here. Instead of immediately conceding that any participant will lie whenever individually profitable, and hence giving up the benefits that result from truthful mutual problem solving, it will be assumed that a norm of telling the truth can be established, and that sanctions can be provided that deter deviation from that norm most of the time. The great advantage of truthfulness is that most lies are discovered eventually. When they are, appropriate payoff adjustments can be made that not only compensate for wrongful payoffs due to the deception, but also include a punitive component. Since the range of possible cooperative payoff division is often quite large, there may be considerable capability to accomplish this adjustment. In other words, it is proposed that the agreed-on welfare function include parameters that achieve the necessary corrections and sanctions for any uncovered past instances of deception, sufficient to make deception an unattractive long-term strategy. Negotiators for victims of cheating would demand welfare functions in accordance with this principle, and arbitrators would uphold them, thereby implementing the principle.

Deception would thereby be inhibited to the extent that deception is likely to be eventually discovered, to the extent that long-term payoff is significant relative to short-term payoff, and to the extent that a cooperative solution has higher payoffs to the potential deceiver than a unilateral solution. All of these conditions apply to relations among nuclear powers, provided the deception is not so significant that one power could thereby permanently dominate another.

III. SUMMARY

When the participants in an encounter can agree on what result would be collectively best (which is obvious in such simple games as Prisoner's Dilemma and Dollar Auction), they can cooperate to achieve that result. Proponents of cooperation can force that result by cooperating with fellow cooperators, deterring potential defectors with minimum-cost sanctions that make defection unprofitable, and treating participants of unknown characteristics as cooperators.

Deciding on collective best can be accomplished in terms of a welfare function with uncertain parameter values to be determined. The various participants might initially propose different parameter values reflecting their different backgrounds and situations. These differences are to be resolved through research applying higher overall principles, negotiation in which the participants try to imagine themselves in each other's situation, and if necessary arbitration by an arbitrator selected for competence and impartiality.

An agreed-on welfare function then lets the participants define collective best. A constraint in going from welfare function to collective best (maximum or satisfied Welfare) is that no participant receive less therefrom than that participant can, or honestly thinks (s)he can, obtain unilaterally. For encounters involving more than two participants, coalitions, if they form at all, have only minor effects, but coalition formation that could lower collective Welfare can likely be deterred. This contrasts with classical n-person game theory, where coalition formation is central.

Whereas *defection* from cooperative choices is to be deterred immediately by minimum-cost sanction moves, *deception,* which distorts the welfare function in favor of the deceiver, is to be deterred by sanctions implemented when the deception is eventually discovered. These sanctions adjust subsequent welfare functions in disfavor of the deceiver sufficiently to make deception unprofitable in the long run.

Overall, the cooperative theory seeks to find the solution to an encounter that is collectively best, as best the participants and if necessary an arbitrator selected by the participants can determine it, and to deter deception and defection by judicious sanctions.

12

ARBITRATION OF MAJOR INTERNATIONAL DISPUTES

In order to avoid war, something must replace it when all currently used other methods for dealing with an international dispute have failed. That something, it is suggested here, is arbitration. A scheme of arbitration, and the reasons why it should work, are presented in Section I of this chapter. The basic characteristics of the proposed scheme are:

1. The issues to be arbitrated include vital interests, particularly those on which the superpowers differ, which might otherwise lead to violent confrontation.

2. The disputing parties agree to arbitration because this process is, and is seen by all parties to be, superior to available alternatives.

3. The disputing parties determine the terms of reference for the arbitration.

4. The disputing parties select impartial, competent arbitrator(s).

5. The disputing parties will accept the arbitration decision, because the decision will have been crafted in such a way that no party can gain by rejecting the decision.

Special attention is given in Section II to means of facilitating the availability of mutually acceptable arbitrators.

While arbitration has frequently been used to resolve minor international disputes, conventional wisdom has been that arbitration could not be used where the vital interests of nations are at stake, because nations should not trust such matters to external determination. It will be shown in Section III that such a view is now unreasonable, and may be a carryover from the times when kings claimed divine rights. Among other counterarguments to be refuted are those related to the need for rational behavior by disputants.

The relationship between the proposed arbitration scheme and proposals for world government is discussed in Section IV. The arbitration scheme should be less difficult to implement because it represents a less drastic change in world organization. A system of international arbitration may, however, evolve into some form of world government.

I. THE SCHEME FOR ARBITRATION

As was discussed in the previous chapter, a difficulty in reaching a negotiated solution to a dispute may be that there are no agreed-on principles pointing to a solution, and an arbitrator may be needed to decide such an issue. Another reason why arbitration might be needed to supplement negotiation, in international disputes as in other disputes, is the reluctance of each party to make concessions during negotiation. A stage of negotiation may be reached where a concession in some sense by one of the parties is needed, but each party would gain by having the other party make the concession, so neither is willing to initiate the process. (Recall the game of Chicken in Chapter 4.) Arbitration resolves this problem. Neither side then needs to make such a concession, to that side's possible disadvantage.

Arbitration of major international disputes, as here proposed, differs from some other applications of arbitration in that there is no superior organization that can enforce the arbitration decision, or even require the parties to undergo arbitration. The arbitration scheme must hence be so crafted, through proper management of informed self-interest, that sovereign nations will agree to utilize it, and agree to abide by the arbitration decision. The reason that they will comply with both these requirements is that all alternatives would be worse for all parties. On the other hand, nations should not be expected to cede to arbitrators, or other external entities, more authority than absolutely essential, and the proposed arbitration scheme meets this requirement.

Arbitration is hence to be initiated when the nations involved in an international dispute, which is not yielding to negotiation, come to the realization that arbitration is the most desirable way to proceed (most cost-effective in the broadest sense of cost). Possible alternatives that arbitration replaces are recriminations and deteriorating relations while the dispute remains unresolved, perhaps with hostile actions to try to compel the other side to give in — the sort of action that in the past has led to war.

Terms of Reference

When disputing parties conclude that arbitration is the best way to proceed with the dispute, they need to determine the terms of reference and to select the arbitrator. Since the decision of the arbitrator presents an uncertainty to the disputing nations, they would want to leave to arbitration only those issues and parameter value ranges that they absolutely cannot resolve in negotiation. Hence, they will seek to narrow the issues as much as possible in prior negotiation, and specify the terms of reference as precisely as possible. The parties can limit the flexibility of arbitrator decisions in any way they choose; they could, for example, allow the arbitrator to select an intermediate value for some disputed parameters, while constraining the arbitrator to choose the position of one side or other, but not an intermediate position, on other issues. (This constraint is known as final offer arbitration, and tends to keep parties from making extreme demands in anticipation that the arbitrator will split the difference.)[1] Failure to agree on any aspect of the terms of reference does not preclude arbitration, but necessitates giving the arbitrator greater decision latitude.

Arbitrator Selection

It is necessary for the parties to agree on the individual(s) or organization to arbitrate the dispute. Since the arbitration scheme has to be workable in the absence of any higher authority, arbitrator selection must be accomplished through agreement by the disputing parties. (Asking another party to select the arbitrators does not eliminate the problem, but merely changes it to the selection of the selector.) As the following explains, negotiation to select arbitrators can be expected to be more tractable than negotiation to solve the original dispute.[2]

The original dispute, which negotiation has been unable to resolve, is likely to contain issues on which positions have hardened and emotions are high, the kind that in the past have led to war. The parties have not been able to find higher principles on which they agree. The selection of arbitrators, on the other hand, involves recognized requirements, that of competence in the subject matter of the issues to be decided, and that of lack of bias. There should not be much conflict of interest between parties in searching for arbitrators who are competent; conflict that arises would more likely be an objection by one party that a particular potential arbitrator is biased in favor of the other party. The search for non-biased arbitrators is not really adversarial; a party could not realistically insist on an arbitrator recognized to be biased in its favor. If there are arbitrators available who are recognized by all parties to be competent and fair, then such an arbitrator will eventually be chosen (perhaps after initial proposals by each party for arbitrators who, that party believes, give it an advantage), since selection of an unbiased arbitrator is preferred by each party to a continuation of the dispute. Some suggestions to enhance the availability of acceptable arbitrators are given in Section II of this chapter.

The arbitration scheme is thus structured to make highly likely the successful selection of arbitrators whenever needed to resolve any specific vital international dispute. Since it is, however, unwise to tolerate even a small possibility of a deadlock in this step, the selection of contingency arbitrators is additionally proposed. This selection would be made by nations as soon as possible after they subscribe to the concept of arbitration of major international disputes, and maintained thereafter. Different contingency arbitrators could be maintained for various pairs of nations and for possible multi-nation dispute groups. Since the contingency arbitrators would likely not be as well suited for a specific dispute as arbitrators specifically selected for such a dispute, there would still be an incentive for nations to select dispute-specific arbitrators, because the latter would be expected to do a better job of maximizing overall welfare. Disputants could hence be expected to agree to arbitrate a dispute with dispute-specific arbitrators at a certain point in the proceedings, but the detriments of the dispute might have to get considerably worse before the parties agree to contingency arbitrators, which one or more parties might fear would yield worse results to it. Since contingency arbitrators would not normally be called upon, and their selection would hence be less contentious, and since they could be chosen at leisure, it should be possible to once establish them, and to perpetuate them thereafter.

Arbitrator Performance

The foremost objective for an arbitrator is acceptance by the disputing parties of the decision rendered. The parties can, of course, ensure this by terms of reference that limit the discretion of the arbitrator so that any decision reached will be preferable to reneging on the agreement to abide by the decision. Where, on the other hand, the parties are unable to narrow the dispute during the negotiating phase and thus have to give wide latitude to the arbitrator, the arbitrator must make sure that the decision will not be so badly received by one of the parties that it might prefer to reject the decision and take unilateral action. The whole premise of negotiation and arbitration is, of course, that an agreement is possible that will leave all sides better off than unilateral action, such as war, and that this agreement can be found. Within satisfying the requirement that the decision will be accepted by all parties, the arbitrator should attempt to reach the decision that, in the arbitrator's view, maximizes the joint welfare of the parties.

Types of Issues Subject to Arbitration

In contrast with international arbitration heretofore attempted,[3] which has not included issues nations deemed of primary importance, it is here proposed that the most vital issues be subject to arbitration. One of the international problems to be solved is arms reduction, leading to the eventual disassembly of the capability of nations to destroy each other. It is perhaps more the acceptance by the nations of the values that the adoption of arbitration would bring to this issue, than calling on arbitrators to make the technical decisions, that would most enhance the accomplishment of this task. If small differences in military capability in various scenarios are perceived as giving nations greater influence relative to other issues, and reductions in military strength must hence be balanced very carefully, progress will be very difficult, as at present. If, on the other hand, it is accepted that disputes will be settled on their merits, and that the only purpose of military strength is to prevent an opposing nation from imposing its will by military action, then there will be much more leeway in the military balance (which is always subject to some uncertainties), and hence arms reduction should be easier to accomplish, whether by negotiation or arbitration.

A class of problems that often have not been solved peacefully, and which could benefit from arbitration, is that related to territory and the appropriate ethnic groupings into governmental units.[4] Consider, for example, the U.S.–Vietnam war. One way of describing it is as a conflict over whether there was to be one government over all Vietnam or separate governments in North and South Vietnam, in which case there was the further conflict over the makeup of the South Vietnam government. The United States insisted on two Vietnams, with a U.S.-supported anticommunist government in the South, largely because it feared that anything else might lead to even further communist expansion. The Communists (i.e., the North Vietnam government and the National Liberation Front) desired a single government for all Vietnam. If free elections for all Vietnam had been held in 1956 as promised, all indications are that a communist government would have been elected.[5] However the Communists apparently would have accepted (in 1964)[6] a split Vietnam with a neutralist government in the South.

Let us speculate what a negotiated or arbitrated outcome might have been if arbitration, as here proposed, had been in vogue in the mid-1960s: perhaps an elected neutralist government in South Vietnam, precluded for x years from rejoining North Vietnam, with x negotiated/arbitrated parameters (thereby giving the United States a respite from an all-communist Vietnam, and some hope that it might not happen at all). Everybody would have been better off, relative not only to what actually happened, but also relative to what the expectations were in 1965.[7] Both sides would have avoided all the losses and other repercussions from fighting the war. The negotiation/arbitration fact-finding would have revealed to the United States both the tenacity of the Vietnamese Communists, making military success more problematical, and the great diversity of objectives among them, the Chinese, and the Soviets, making further communist expansion less likely. Surely, the fall of the rest of the countries of Southeast Asia to Com-munism (the domino theory), which did not occur after the actual communist takeover of Vietnam, would not have occurred after an arbitration settle-ment. The main U.S. reason for engaging in hostili-ties in Vietnam, maintaining credibility in opposing Communist expansion, would have been served just as well by contesting by means of arbitration as by means of war.

The U.S.–Vietnam conflict, and how arbitration might have prevented the war, are described in greater detail in the Appendix.

The Camp David Accord between Egypt and Israel, where Israel agreed to return territory to Egypt, and Egypt agreed to recognize Israel, is another example of the type of dispute for which the arbitration approach might be appropriate. The procedure by which agreement was actually reached, through mediation by U.S. President Carter, was really not much different from the proposed arbitration approach. A single-text procedure was used, where the U.S. mediators listened to both sides, prepared a draft, repeatedly asked for criticism to obtain improved drafts, and when they presented the ultimate text as the best that could be done, both sides accepted. The proposed arbitration process would only be different in that the disputing parties would agree in advance to accept the best text that the third party could devise, and that normally the third party would not be the president of a more powerful country than the disputants, and that hence the disputants would have greater responsibility to initiate and control the process.

Legal Framework

Once parties submit an international dispute to arbitration, they are committed to accept the arbitration decision. Hence, any national ratification processes need to be accomplished prior to the submission of the dispute to arbitration. For example, the agreement to submit a dispute to binding arbitration, together with the terms of reference and the arbitrators selected, might be considered to constitute a treaty, and hence in the United States subject to approval by two-thirds of the Senate. It is interesting to note that declaration of war, requiring only a majority of the two houses of Congress (to say nothing of direct presidential authority to get the country involved in hostilities), is less difficult than treaty ratification. Perhaps the time will come when the imbalance can be reversed, to make ratification of agreements easier than approval of hostilities.

II. FACILITATION OF AVAILABILITY OF ACCEPTABLE ARBITRATORS

The availability of arbitrators acceptable to disputing parties is a key requirement of the arbitration scheme. Two suggestions to help facilitate the availability of acceptable arbitrators are made in this section, namely the establishment of an international institute for the training of arbitrators, and the establishment of multiple organizations to compete in making arbitration decisions that, in retrospect, will be found to have been the wisest.

Arbitration Institute

There are two purposes to establishing an international institute for the training of arbitrators. One is the selection of qualified candidates and their training. The other is the monitoring of the arbitrator candidates by a faculty including trusted representatives of the nations that might call on the services of arbitrators. These faculty members could satisfy themselves and their government that individual graduates of the institute would be competent and fair in arbitrating their nation's disputes.

Arbitrators need to understand the values and backgrounds of the parties whose disputes they are to resolve. Faculty members could teach the values and backgrounds of the nations they represent, and make sure their trainees absorbed this information. The faculty members would be able to observe their trainees closely, to learn their trainees' biases, and to assure themselves that any such biases would not interfere with the ability to make fair decisions. (It should be understood that "trainee" here implies neither youth nor lack of prior accomplishment; distinction in related fields might well be a prerequisite for admission to the arbitrator institute.) When nations are considering the selection of specific arbitrators for an international dispute they would consult with faculty members of the arbitrator institute who are familiar with them.

The arbitrator institute would, of course, do more than merely instruct in the values and backgrounds of various nations. The arbitrators would be expected to become knowledgeable in the issues surrounding disputes and in looking for solutions to maximize the welfare of their clients. Since arbitration in the absence of enforcement powers takes on many of the characteristics of single-text mediation, the arbitrators would also have to become skilled in mediation techniques. The institute would also be engaged in research to improve dispute-resolution techniques.

Multiple Arbitration Organizations

It has been shown that in many situations (e.g., Prisoner's Dilemma game, overcoming deception) performance can be improved if the process is extended over many repetitions. The same principle may hold in arbitrator choice. It may be possible to judge the soundness of an arbitrator's decisions in retrospect, and then use this evaluation to help in the selection of arbitrators to resolve subsequent disputes. To be able to judge arbitrators over a sufficient length of time and over sufficiently numerous decisions, it is perhaps better to establish arbitration organizations rather than individual arbitrators, since such organizations can exist longer and better establish a reputation. It is suggested that a significant number of arbitration organizations be encouraged and funded internationally. (The costs, though not inconsiderable, would be trivial compared to those of armaments and wars.) The arbitration organizations would compete to establish the best reputations regarding the soundness of their arbitration decisions.

To enhance this competition, all leading arbitration organizations could be asked to participate in all major international arbitrations and to arrive at individual decisions. These various decisions need not all be utilized in settling the dispute for which they are reached, but all would be put on record and used in subsequent evaluations of the organizations, for those instances where later hindsight allows judgment of the quality of the decisions. (Where there is a dispute among nations about such a judgment, the process for the resolution of international disputes here proposed could be used for that dispute as well. Of course, different agencies and individuals would handle this particular task.)

Disputing nations would have choices in determining how to combine the arbitration decisions reached by the various arbitration organizations called in on a case. They could decide to use only the decision reached by one arbitration organization, or they could decide to utilize some weighted combination of the decisions by various of the organizations. Particularly attractive would be a combination of the decisions of the participating arbitration organizations weighted according to the judgment of the soundness of their various previous decisions.

The attitude here advocated is that arbitrators be looked upon as impartial experts, to be called upon to help disputing parties resolve the uncertainties that are keeping them from determining the solution that maximizes their common welfare. Where the experts disagree, those should be favored who have demon-strated the greatest success in the past. Moreover, a system coupling the relative influence of arbitration organizations to the quality of past decisions tends to foster honesty. Suppose that a party in a dispute gets a decision biased in its favor by deceiving some arbi-trators. When the deception is eventually discovered, the arbitrators who were deceived are downrated and will in the future have less influence, thereby leaving future decisions in the hands of arbitrators who are less receptive to the arguments of the party that engaged in the earlier deception.

It should be noted that coupling arbitration influence to the quality of arbitration decision requires a welfare-based decision criterion, as is strongly recommended in this book, rather than a threat-based criterion. For example, if a decision is based on which party would prevail in a war, and the decision is accepted and there is no war, then subsequent history cannot help decide whether the arbitrator judged the parties' strengths correctly. (If there is war, allowing the arbitrator's threat-based decision to be judged, then the arbitration system has of course failed.)

III. OVERCOMING PERCEIVED LIMITATIONS ON INTERNATIONAL ARBITRATION

The ideas presented in the two previous sections are meant to complement, and perhaps supercede, presently available facilities for third party assistance in the peaceful resolution of international disputes. There have been many successful international arbitrations in the past (see Note 3) — but not of the major international disputes. The International Court of Justice exists to arbitrate disputes that nations bring to it — but even though nations have many disputes that they cannot resolve peacefully, the Court is little used. "Everybody knows that nations have resisted third-party settlements of their disputes and that adjudicative techniques thus far have played a very limited role in their relations."[8] For example, in "The Role and Problems of Arbitration with Respect to Political Disputes," Dean Rusk states without further justification that "Many issues seem to be too vital in the security or other national interests of the contending parties to be submitted to third-party determination."[9] We must hence inquire why arbitration of international disputes is perceived to be so limited, and show how the proposed arbitration approach overcomes these limitations.

One authority, Bilder (see Note 8), finds two main justifications for the reluctance to arbitrate vital issues: for any of a number of reasons, a third party might reach a wrong decision; and an arbitral decision based on narrow judicial grounds may not be the best solution to a conflict. It will be shown below that these concerns should not preclude the proposed arbitration scheme. Some critics to whom I have described the proposed approach have suggested additionally that it is dependent on a degree of rationality that does not exist in the real world; this objection will also be addressed. Finally, it will be suggested that reluctance to arbitrate has a historical basis, which today is no longer relevant.

Welfare Arbitration vs. Judicial Arbitration

The answer to the concern that arbitration based on narrow judicial grounds may not yield the best resolution to a dispute is that in the proposed arbitration scheme, arbitration is not to be limited to judicial bodies, such as the International Court of Justice. There are, of course, many disputes where judicial solutions are suitable, for example, disputes on interpretation of treaty provisions, and for these the parties might select a judicial body as arbitrator. (A judicial solution determines which available laws are relevant and attempts to apply them to the situation at hand.) However, many disputes involve a clash of values, which has not heretofore been resolved, for which resolution cannot be attained through examination of existing law, and for which legal training may not be the best preparation. It is for this reason that the scheme provides latitude for disputing nations to procure arbitrators who can fashion solutions that achieve the best overall welfare of the parties to the dispute, and which each party understands would be counterproductive to reject.

Who Can Achieve the Best Solution?

The concern that a third party might reach a wrong decision is answered in a similar manner. To the extent that negotiating parties can resolve their dispute by themselves, with or without non-binding help from outside sources, they should of course do so. Where they do need arbitrators, the better the disputing nations can define the problem between themselves, and the better they can select suitable arbitrators, the smaller the chances for a bad decision by the arbitrators. However much leeway remains for the arbitrators, the whole thrust of the scheme is to use that process that will come up with the best solution. Surely a war (even neglecting its cost) or a gladiatorial contest (even assuming the parties would abide by its results) would not generally yield a better solution than a reasoned decision by carefully selected arbitrators. A better alternative does not exist.

Arbitration and Rationality

The arbitration approach requires that an arbitration decision be reached which each party clearly prefers to what that party could get in the absence of the arbitration decision. This places constraints on the decision that the arbitrator can make that will be accepted, as was developed in the previous chapter. The arbitrator must forego making a decision outside that constraint even when such a decision would result in higher overall welfare. The arbitrator must be sufficiently understanding to judge the limits of the range in which a decision is thus acceptable.

The only "rationality" required of a disputing party is that it accept an outcome it likes better over one it likes less, which can safely be assumed to exist. Of course, a party's values and preferences might differ, even radically, from our values, but that does not preclude the arbitration process. Sufficiently gross misperception (when the arbitrator has been unable to relieve it) by at least one of the parties of the true situation could in some disputes make it impossible for an arbitrator to reach a decision preferred by both parties to a unilateral solution; but where the unilateral solution is war, the benefit of an arbitrated agreement would be so great that no amount of misperception could exhaust the range where the arbitrator's decision would be acceptable.[10]

Hence, no special rationality is required of the disputants for arbitration to work, and the greater the benefits to be derived from arbitration in a particular situation, the smaller its chance of failure because of misperceptions by the disputants.

Why the Reluctance to Arbitrate?

We have examined a number of arguments against arbitration of major international disputes and found them not to be valid. Besides international disputes, life is full of situations where disputes are submitted to arbitrators or similar third parties. Legislatures, voters, judges, and juries are bodies that make third-party decisions about disputes. Government officials and lawyers, in particular, often have their vital issues decided by such bodies. Why then the reluctance to have international issues also decided by arbitration? One would not think that government officials really prefer to stake their success on a superior armed force rather than on a superior arbitration position (e.g., lose a Vietnam war rather than lose a Vietnam arbitration, if each outcome is equally likely).

There may, however, be a historical explanation for the reluctance to arbitrate major international disputes.[11] It has to do with the divine rights of kings. The monarchs of Europe in and around the eighteenth century could not afford to give up to international arbitrators the control of vital policies for their kingdoms, without calling into question their rights to rule their kingdoms. To them, war was a more desirable decision alternative, being essentially a duel fought by professional armies, designed to merely settle the dispute and not to annihilate the losing state. The reluctance to accept international arbitration of vital issues may be a relic of those days.

IV. ARBITRATION VIS-A-VIS WORLD GOVERNMENT

The only other alternative to the present ways of controlling international conflict through a precarious balance of power, or the proposed system of international arbitration, is one of variously proposed schemes for a supranational authority, under world law, that would have superior enforcement power. A typical example of this approach is summarized below. The major advantage here claimed for the arbitration approach over the supranational authority is that the arbitration approach should be much easier to implement; the difficulty of establishing a supranational authority will be compared to the relative simplicity of implementing arbitration. The two approaches are, however, not mutually exclusive; this section will conclude with a speculation of how a system of international arbitration might be the very means of developing world government.

A Typical Proposal for World Government

A typical proposal calls for a federal world government with the following essentials:[12]

1. a bill of rights,
2. a popularly elected legislature to enact world laws,
3. a world court to interpret those laws, with compulsory jurisdiction over world disputes,
4. a civilian executive branch with the power to enforce world laws directly upon individuals,
5. a system of checks and balances to prevent the abuse of power by any branch of world government,
6. the control of all weapons of mass destruction by the world government, with the disarmament of all nations, under careful inspection down to the level required for internal policing,
7. carefully defined and limited power of taxation to support those functions necessary to world peace and the solution of problems affecting, to a vital degree, the welfare of all mankind,
8. reasonable provision for amendments,
9. participation in the world federal government to be open at all times to all nations, and

10. all power not expressly delegated to the world government to be reserved to the nations and their peoples, thus leaving each nation to choose its own political, social, and economic system.

If the United Nations were to be used as the vehicle for world government, a thoroughgoing revision of its charter would be required. The United Nations presently cannot force a major nation, particularly one (the United States, the Soviet Union, China, Great Britain, or France) having veto power in the Security Council, to do anything against its will, and hence cannot prevent war. With or without the veto, the UN in its present form cannot resolve a conflict if the major powers disagree.

The present situation has been compared to the American Confederation of States prior to the 1787 Constitutional Convention, and it has been suggested that it can be handled in an analogous way.[13] Note the similarity between the proposed world constitution outlined above and the constitution of the United States. It has been further suggested that world constitutional convention analogous to the Constitutional Convention of 1787 could bring about a world government. We are reminded of the many difficulties faced and overcome in arriving at the U.S. Constitution. The Articles of Confederation were not working well, states had their own armed forces and coinage, they taxed each other, and there were armed confrontations. At the Convention, they had to overcome many conflicts, most notably those about the relative representation of large and small states, and about slavery. Yet, the work of the Constitutional Convention of 1787 turned out to be a success (with one flaw — the Civil War — which would have to be avoided this time around).

Differences

We must, on the other hand, recognize the many differences between the problem of creating a federal government for the 13 states of the American Confederation of 1787 and creating a world government of the more than 150 sovereign nations of today. Of the differences, perhaps the one that presents the greatest obstacle is that the sovereign nations of the world have operated that way for generations and the inhabitants have adapted to the situation, whereas the American States had operated as a confederation for only a few years, and in a manner that was generally recognized as unsatisfactory.

Well-known proposals for world government have been around for over 30 years,[14] and do not appear to have made much headway. Apparently, the change from national allegiance to world allegiance is too great to be supported soon by either public opinion or government leaders. The establishment of world government would bring about drastic changes, the consequences of which are not fully predictable with even the best preparation.

The scheme for international arbitration, on the other hand, is *an approach to prevent war with the minimum changes required to accomplish that purpose.* Other than providing a decision mechanism to replace hostile confrontation and war, and a consequent decrease in war psychology and pressure for military expenditures, the arbitration approach does not require changes in the present conduct of society. Therefore, it should be easier to attain adoption of international arbitration than of world government, and it is for this reason that the proposed international arbitration approach may be the most promising path to peace.

Blending Arbitration and World Government

Aside from the advantage of international arbitration constituting a lesser change in world organization, and hence having a better chance than world government of being adopted in the foreseeable future, how do these approaches to a world without war compare, and can we combine the best features of each? If international arbitration is first adopted along the lines suggested here, then those components of world government proposals that are advantageous might be adopted much more readily than in the present environment.

The arbitration approach is designed to come up with solutions to disputes that provide the maximum overall satisfaction and the greatest chance that they will be satisfactory to all parties. Thus, a relatively involved decision process has been proposed, includ-ing issue negotiation between representatives of disputing nations, arbitrator development, arbitrator selection by the disputants, negotiation on terms of reference by the disputants, the most careful attain-able arbitration process to leave no justification for noncompliance, and post-arbitration analysis to correct any imperfections of the process by feedback into future arbitrations. Such a process might often be more cumbersome than an executive, legislative, or judicial decision of a more conventional government. Hence, as confidence is gained with decisions made by arbitrators, it might be found expedient to streamline those decisions, such as by retaining arbitrators of specific expertise indefinitely, and by letting some issues be decided directly by such arbitrators (who thereby become world government officials) rather than via prolonged preliminary negotiation. In other words, world government could supercede arbitration in those matters where a central government could better perform the job. The arbitration process would then be reserved for the most sensitive issues, where opinions are still polarized and where the most deliberate decision process is justified. It is hence suggested, to advocates of world government that support of the proposed scheme for international arbitration may be the best strategy for eventually achieving world government.

The best balance between the extremes of doing no more than adding an arbitration system to the present international arrangement, and the more classical scheme of world government, is a matter that can be determined as we gain experience in settling issues with the aid of such an arbitration system. I would like to point to one aspect, however, where it might be desirable to stop short of going all the way from an arbitration system to the classically proposed form of world government. That is with respect to a world police force. A typical classical scheme[15] calls for a world police force that, after universal national disarmament down to internal police forces, would be clearly superior in armament and troops to the police force of any nation or likely coalition of nations. In spite of safeguards to be provided, a danger of such an arrangement is that some inimical faction could gain control of the world police force, and thereby impose its will on the world. With the arbitration system, on the other hand, nations would simply disarm in a verified balanced way, with no world police force; illegal armament could be deterred (beyond the usual ways of deterring defection) by contingency arrangements to combine national residual forces against such a violation. A world police force could create a climate where problems could be resolved by the establishment imposing its will on dissenters; with no world police force, the necessary effort to resolve differences by negotiation and arbitration would have to be made.

13

GETTING TO PEACE

Having seen how we can and why we must now eliminate war, we examine in this final chapter some steps we can take to help getting to peace, or to get there quickly, and some of the traps to avoid. Section I of this chapter describes some policies that impede peace, how they should be changed, and how such changes can in particular help in the control and reduction of arms. Section II reviews what can work in establishing peace, and how in the process of achieving peace we can solve our other societal problems as well. The concluding part, Section III, focuses on the part the individual can play in supporting peace. Just as everybody gains when a dispute is resolved by a sound agreement, so can the individual support peace in such a way that the activity is pleasant as well as rewarding.

I. TRAPS TO AVOID, AND SOME OBVIOUS ARMS CONTROL STEPS

The title of this book, "Peace Through Agreement," is meant to contrast with another philosophy that is widely propounded, namely, peace through strength. There is, of course, nothing wrong with being strong enough so that no potential opponent can profit by attacking you or those whom you have an obligation to protect; that is, in fact, clearly required by the theory in this book. The objection comes when the strength is used to force adoption of your views over other views in a dispute, instead of being merely sufficiently strong to force a fair, peaceful resolution. The strength required for the former application is obviously much greater. There are a number of things wrong with peace through strength.

In the first place, all a single nation can control is its absolute strength, not its strength relative to a confronting nation. If two opposing nations both adopt the peace through strength approach, then neither has gained anything; their relative strength is likely still the same. Both, however, have lost a lot. They have expended a lot of resources in increasing their strength, resources that could otherwise have been used to improve the well-being of their people. They have also developed a military psychology and a temptation to use the strength they have worked so hard to achieve.

Even if a peace through strength program does strengthen the nation adopting it relative to another, that is not necessarily a good thing. It would be a good thing only if the stronger nation behaves more responsibly. The opposite has probably occurred more often throughout history. The problem, of course, is that each of the opposing nations believes itself to be the worthier one, and the other one (or its government) the one in need of, at least, modification.

Some claim it was the success of a U.S. policy of peace through strength that led to recent Soviet moves of unilateral and bilateral arms reduction, and to a less confrontational Soviet attitude. I would characterize it differently: In the game of nuclear chicken that the major powers have for too long been playing, it was the Soviet side, with the accession of Mikhail Gorbachev, that first realized the futility of the game (perhaps because the Soviets were suffering more from it), and hence made the necessary first concession to try to end the game. It is being borne out that whatever small loss in relative position such a first concession entails, it is vastly outweighed by the resulting benefits to everyone. Now that a conciliatory process has started, for whatever reason, it would be unfortunate indeed if we do not embrace it fully, but jeopardize it with a peace through strength policy that could impede the peace process or even bring it to a halt.

There is a variation on the theme of peace through strength weakness of which is even more obvious, namely that we should negotiate disputes, but not just now. Wait until our position is a little stronger, until we have won just one more battle, until the other side meets an additional precondition, until we have developed, or perfected, or funded, another weapon system. Or let us build another weapon system or two, so that we can trade away an existing one in arms control negotiations.

Again, there are two possible results. The improvement we sought may prove illusory. The battle was not won, but both sides have suffered more losses and more people have become embittered. Or both sides have increased their arms level, at much cost to each of them. The power relation has not changed, but the dispute has become more difficult to resolve.

Or suppose we are successful in improving our position. The other side may now be willing to accede to the terms we demanded but were unable to attain before. But will we be satisfied with that? Of course not. Now that our position has improved, we want correspondingly better terms. The negotiating gap has not closed. Only complete victory will close the gap, and victory is not possible in the nuclear age.

For an example, see in the Appendix the section on how the war in Vietnam actually happened, how time and time again the conclusion was reached that time was not yet ripe for negotiation.

There is only one answer as to when to negotiate: NEGOTIATE NOW. There is never a better time. Any prospective actions by any party that might affect the outcome can be considered in the negotiation. If highly trained arbitrators are developed as proposed in Chapter 12, then these can provide the world's best estimate as to how steps by the parties to improve their positions might have fared. It will not be necessary to actually fight the battles, or to actually build the bargaining chips. Of course, as also recommended in Chapter 12, agreements should be based on common welfare as much as possible, and on power and position of the parties only to the extent that the parties could prevail if they acted unilaterally.

In addition to the stopping of ongoing fighting, early priority should be given to those phases of arms production that are environmentally damaging. This was done in the case of atmospheric testing of nuclear weapons. It seems that producing more plutonium and tritium for nuclear warheads will be environmentally polluting, or very expensive, or both. In an era of arms reduction, there seems to be little to be said for not negotiating a treaty to stop the production of nuclear warhead fuels. In the case of tritium, which decays at the rate of 5.5 percent per year, the natural reduction in its stockpile, if new production were cut off, might nicely match and enhance other phases of arms reduction.

One further high priority item that ought to be, but appears not to be, on arms control agreement agendas is as complete a limitation as possible on research and development of new or improved weapons. It may not be possible to ban all such research because of verification difficulties (although we might overcome some of those if we really put our minds to it), but that does not excuse not impeding weapon research and development, by agreement, wherever possible. Any weapon tests in the atmosphere and in space are detectable and can therefore be forbidden. It is just common sense that while reducing and eliminating existing weapons, we should try to avoid the proliferation of new ones. With respect to claims that some weapon improvements lead to more stable and hence safer opposing weapon systems, development of such improvements could be turned over to international teams, whose tasks would be limited to facilitating more stable opposing weapon systems, without giving any nation a significant advantage.

II. TO ACHIEVE PEACE AND MORE

War has been ascribed to many causes, but, in a sense, there is only one cause: failure to resolve a dispute by peaceful means. A universally accepted method for the peaceful resolution of disputes can prevent war. The objective of this book has been to present such a method. A feature of this method is that it does not depend at all on the use of force —

anybody's force — but depends instead on the proper management of self-interest. At every stage of the process, the global benefit accruing from a peaceful resolution is divided up so that everyone partakes of it, and that no one can gain from disrupting the process. Negotiation and arbitration are important parts of the process.

With the availability of such a method, the blame for any hostilities will be clearly with the party that refuses to seek a fair solution by negotiation, and if necessary arbitration, of any dispute. Defense of the status quo does not, in any way, lessen the responsibility of a party to engage in the negotiation and arbitration process with a challenging party. The motivation for this analysis is, of course, not to assess blame, but to define responsibilities. The above reasoning can be extended to assert that in *any* war, past wars included, *at least* one of the participants is wrong to engage in it, and possibly all.

The scheme proposed in this book can do more than just prevent war. As a byproduct of devising dispute solutions that have the greatest chance of acceptance, the proposed solutions are also designed to be the best that humankind can devise. In other words, what has been proposed is a best method for solving *any* societal problem. For problems that are on a less than international scale, the magnitude of the resolution effort can be scaled down correspondingly. With the availability of a means of having grievances resolved on their merits, no group would have the need, nor the excuse, to engage in violent confrontation.

War is only the most extreme example of destructive conflict. There are other ways of harming a rival than through physical violence. A conflict can be considered destructive whenever the joint welfare is intentionally reduced by one or more of the parties in a dispute over payoff distribution. The proposed dispute-resolution approach is applicable to such disputes as well.

The benefits from the elimination of war, and preparation for war, are so great that it should be readily possible to have everyone share in the benefits. If some segments of society believe that they will lose from such steps toward peace as arms reduction and disarmament, they might obstruct the process, thereby making its success less likely. In order to prevent this from happening, it is necessary to have credible plans of how those who are now in defense-related activities can change to other activities at no loss in well-being. And to do that, it is necessary to have national-scale plans on the activities that will take the place of eliminated defense work, in such a way that the freed-up workers and their talents will be fully utilized. There is certainly enough work that society needs done to fully utilize all the human and other resources that would become available. Making those plans well ahead of the actual shift from military to civilian activities, preferably immediately, will facilitate reaching agreement on large-scale arms control and disarmament. The topic has received attention under the heading of conversion (distinguished from "reconversion," which was the process that followed World War II).[1]

III. PLEASANT WAYS TO SUPPORT PEACE

The problem of supporting peace can be considered to be a non-zero-sum game between peace advocates and the remainder of the population, who are less committed or not at all committed to peace. And just as peace among nations is to be attained by a joint welfare maximizing process by the nations, using peaceful dispute-resolution methods, so might disputes between peace advocates and the remainder of the population be resolved by a peaceful process through which both benefit. Peace support can be beneficial to its advocates as well as to the rest of society. In fact, using this approach to convince skeptics that this approach is worthy might be the best strategy for convincing them. The process can also be cumulative — the more peace advocates there are, the easier it should be to convince the dwindling remainder of the population. This is somewhat analogous to the example in Chapter 5, where the larger the fraction of the population that are cooperators, the greater is the relative (as well as absolute) payoff to cooperators; when the fraction of cooperators is large enough, it is advantageous for all defectors to convert and become cooperators.

The key to peace advocacy, as well as to the attainment of peace among nations, is the understanding of non-zero-sum principles and their application to the problems faced by individuals and by society. The cause of war, and of many lesser difficulties, is the failure to properly apply non-zero-sum approaches to conflicts. One indication of how addicted we are to zero-sum thinking is that the games played by the general population are almost all zero-sum. The mathematical theory of games began with zero-sum games; game theorists, who might otherwise lead us in the application of non-zero-sum theory toward peace, have not yet fully escaped the zero-sum origins of game theory. (It is, of course, hoped that this book will help toward that end.)

It is for these reasons that consideration of non-zero-sum games has been such a central part of this book. Those who would like to help advance the cause of peace can do so by spreading the understanding of non-zero-sum principles. One specific way to accomplish this is to play the non-zero-sum games presented in this book: NZS Scrabble, NZS bridge, and NZS basketball. Playing such non-zero-sum games could create greater understanding and awareness of non-zero-sum principles among players and observers of these games, thereby aiding the cause of peace. Playing such games requires no sacrifice from the players; indeed, these games might prove more interesting than the conventional zero-sum versions.

Another way to help is to learn and make use of non-zero-sum principles in your own life, including techniques of negotiation, mediation, and arbitration; be a cooperator. In addition to fostering an environment favoring the spread of non-zero-sum principles, you might, as the theory of this book suggests, increase your own payoffs. Insist, of course, that people you elect, and others with whom you have influence, understand and utilize non-zero-sum principles, and that they support achieving peace through agreement, replacing war with non-violent dispute-resolution methods.

APPENDIX: HOW ARBITRATION MIGHT HAVE PREVENTED THE U.S.–VIETNAM WAR

The purpose of this appendix is to illustrate the proposed process for the arbitration of major international disputes by applying it retrospectively to a historical dispute, namely to the one which led to the U.S. military intervention in Vietnam. A historical rather than a current dispute has been selected for the arbitration example because a premature analysis of a dispute by someone advocating arbitration, particularly by one not privy to all the pertinent facts (which would be available to an agreed-on arbitrator), could cause that person to be perceived as an advocate of a particular position. The focus of the example would shift from an inquiry into the efficacy of arbitration to the merits of the particular analysis of the dispute. Furthermore, new developments could cause a discussion of a current dispute to become quickly dated. The facts are much more available for a historical dispute, especially one as extensively examined as that of Vietnam.

Section I of this appendix consists of a brief description of the author's interpretation of what happened in Vietnam. Section II describes how the scenario might have been different if arbitration of major international disputes had then been in vogue. This difference is the crux of the case for the workability of arbitration. If national leaders (and public opinion) view the world in terms of military confrontation, then they will seek military solutions for real or imagined problems. If, on the other hand, diplomatic solutions are expected, then leaders can pursue these rather than military confrontation without being perceived as weak. With arbitration in vogue, it is very possible that arbitration might not have been needed, and that agreement could have been reached by negotiation alone. Section III indicates why the process, once begun, would likely have led to a peaceful resolution of the dispute, and what the nature of the solution might have been.

I. THE VIETNAM CONFLICT AS IT ACTUALLY HAPPENED

It is generally agreed that the reason for the U.S. intervention in Vietnam was the insistence by the United States on the creation and maintenance of an anticommunist state in South Vietnam, which was unacceptable to North Vietnam and to many South Vietnamese who eventually comprised the NLF (National Liberation Front) (Kahin 1986; Karnow 1983; Ball 1982, part VII; Tuchman 1984). The Geneva accords of 1954 following the defeat of the French at Dienbienphu had provided for a temporary division of Vietnam, with the Veitminh (Communist) forces in control in the North and the French in control in the South, with nationwide elections to be held in 1956. Since a Communist victory in such an election was likely, the United States helped South Vietnam's ruler Diem to prevent the election, knowing that this was likely to lead to renewed hostilities and that the United States might consequently have to intervene militarily in Vietnam (Kahin 1986, 88–92).

Such hostilities indeed developed, and by 1964 material help and U.S. military advisors were no longer sufficient to maintain control of South Vietnam by the Diem government or a number of succeeding governments established through coups supported by the United States. Following a trumped-up incident in the Gulf of Tonkin, leading to a congressional resolution authorizing President Johnson to further intervene (Kahin 1986, 219–25), the United States began bombing raids on North Vietnam in August 1964, and started sending ground combat troops to South Vietnam in March 1965. Further escalation by both sides followed. U.S troops in South Vietnam exceeded 500,000 by the end of the Johnson administration in January 1969. U.S troops were gradually withdrawn during the Nixon administration, but bombing of North Vietnam was increased and the war was caused to spread into Cambodia and Laos. A ceasefire between the United States and North Vietnam went into effect in January 1973; fighting between the Vietnamese soon resumed, and ended in April 1975 with the Communist occupation of Saigon.

A number of efforts were made to initiate negotiation to settle the conflict (Karnow 1983, 491–98), but they never got very far. Perhaps the best opportunity occurred in the period July 1964 through April 1965, following a call by U.N. Secretary General

U Thant for negotiation, which was supported by French President de Gaulle as well as Moscow, Peking, Phnom Pen, Hanoi, and the NLF (Kahin 1986, 215). U Thant subsequently secured Hanoi's agreement for bilateral talks with the United States, but the United States rejected the proposal (Kahin 1986, 243–45). Johnson's advisors (with the exception of George Ball) continually admonished that negotiation was unthinkable until Saigon could bargain politically and militarily from a position of greater strength — strength sufficient to ensure its survival as a separate, noncommunist state (Kahin 1986, 322). As one reads about policy on negotiation (Kahin 1986, 137, 241, 312, 324, 328, 331, 357, 400; Karnow 1983, 193, 334, 484, 496, 629, 640), it is striking how time and time again the conclusion is drawn that the time is not yet ripe for negotiation, that some further military successes are needed to bring bargaining power in line with bargaining demands (as if the demands did not move elusively in lockstep with perceived strength). As the United States invested increasing resources in Vietnam, the greater U.S. objective in Vietnam became to avoid a humiliating U.S. defeat (Kahin 1986, 312–13).

The Vietnam war turned out to be costly for all sides. Three million Americans served in Vietnam, 58,000 were killed, and many veterans suffered from post-traumatic stress disorder and other problems. U.S. expenditures for Vietnam from 1965 to 1973 totaled more than $120 billion, and were responsible for inflation and contributed to the relative decline of the United States in the world economy. The United States had arguably lost a war for the first time in its history. Its ability for subsequent military intervention in the future had been constrained. (This is not all bad.) As South Vietnam ambassador to the United

States Bui Diem said, "Small nations must be wary of the Americans, since U.S. policies shift quickly as domestic policies and public opinion change" (Karnow 1983, 21). Yet, some of the dire consequences (e.g., the domino theory, that nations would fall to the Communists one by one), which were predicted to follow a Communist takeover of Vietnam, did not occur. Except for Laos and Cambodia (which the United States had caused to be involved in the war), no other Southeast Asian nations were taken over by the Communists.

Vietnam was reunified under a Communist government; however, 11 years of separation under different regimes made reintegration difficult. Out of a population of about 40 million, North and South Vietnam suffered over 4 million casualties, including 700,000 killed. The war left Vietnam impoverished and without sufficient food, and many left Vietnam as refugees. Cambodians suffered much more; about 2 million Cambodians (about one-fourth of the population) died in a genocide perpetrated by the Pol Pot regime that had taken over that country.

II. ARBITRATION SCENARIO

Assume now that the proposal for arbitration of major international disputes had been generally agreed to by most nations, as well as incorporated into their constitutions and laws and supported by public opinion. Let us further assume that in July 1964, the time at which U.N. Secretary General U Thant had actually attempted to initiate negotiations, U Thant had invoked the arbitration understanding, declaring that a major international dispute existed, and calling upon the parties to negotiate, with the understanding that issues that could not be resolved by negotiation would be arbitrated. The question we first need to answer is whether, under these circumstances, the negotiation/arbitration process could have gotten started, in contrast to the actual course of events in which the United States refused to negotiate. A positive answer to this question is developed below; the prognosis for such negotiation/arbitration is discussed in Section III.

Communist agreement to participate in a negotiation/arbitration process can be assumed, since they were willing to enter into negotiations in 1964 in the actual situation. For example, "in early September 1964, the U.N. secretary general secured Hanoi's agreement to direct bilateral talks with the United States" (Kahin 1986, 243). Some time later, a staff assessment prepared for McGeorge Bundy (an advisor to President Johnson) regarding North Vietnamese negotiating proposals concluded, "If we choose to make them so, [North Vietnam Premier] Pham Van Dong's proposals could provide the basis for a negotiating dialog" (Kahin 1986, 326).

There are two reasons to believe that President Johnson would have agreed to try negotiation/arbitration under the arbitration scenario, thereby enabling this process. One is specific to the Vietnam situation, and the other applies to the negotiation/arbitration process in general. About the specific Vietnam situation, President Johnson was not at all eager to become involved in a Vietnam war, but believed the alternative to be worse, namely the spread of Communism in Southeast Asia and a consequent weakening of the U.S. position vis-à-vis the Communists throughout the world, because U.S. credibility to protect other nations against Communism might thereby be lost, and these nations might in turn succumb. A March 1965 analysis in Defense Secretary

McNamara's office weighted U.S. objectives in Vietnam as "70% To avoid a humiliating U.S. defeat (to our reputation as a guarantor), 20% To keep SVN [South Vietnam] (and the adjacent) territory from Chinese hands, 10% To permit the people of SVN to enjoy a better, freer way of life" (Kahin 1986, 313). And even though the U.S. administration members continually overestimated the effectiveness of its military initiatives in Vietnam, they were aware that the initiatives could fail. For example, a July 1965 estimate in the Defense Department gave only a 50 percent probability of success by 1968 with the introduction of 200,000 to 400,000 plus U.S. troops (Kahin 1986, 357).

In the arbitration scenario, the 70 percent reason, avoiding a humiliating defeat, would have gone away, since arbitration, not war, would have been the accepted mode of behavior. Nobody could then have accused the United States of being humiliated for following expected behavior and trying arbitration before going to war. (The United States refused conventional negotiation because it believed, perhaps wrongly, that this would have no chance of success and some risk in South Vietnamese morale.) Regarding the 20 percent reason, avoiding Communist expansion in Southeast Asia, there is no reason to assume that impartial arbitrators would have given the Communists more than those arbitrators believed could be obtained through a military conflict (almost by definition of impartial arbitration). The 10 percent reason, a better life for the Vietnamese people, surely would have been better served by arbitration than by a brutal war in Vietnam.

The more general reason for assuming that the arbitration process would have been initiated, is one of expectation and institutionalization. By 1964, aggressive opposition to Communism was the standard U.S. policy, and making the concessions that would have been necessary to reach a negotiated settlement would have been politically risky. If, however, public opinion and the law favored the use of arbitration rather than armed force, there would have been no reason for the Johnson administration not to attempt the arbitration route. The prospects for arbitration would be enhanced if constitutional and legislative changes were made requiring an attempt at arbitration, where feasible, prior to the use of military force. It should not be easier for a president to go to war than to go to arbitration. (The results of either would be binding on the country.)

One factor, which created a climate favoring military action in the original Vietnam situation, was that the United States had never lost a war, and once U.S. forces were involved, no president wanted to be the first to lose a conflict. That impediment toward negotiation and arbitration now no longer applies.

III. POSSIBLE RESULTS OF NEGOTIATION/ARBITRATION

It was hypothesized in the previous section that a world-view that arbitration of major international disputes should be tried in preference to military action would have been sufficient to get a negotiation/arbitration process started in the Vietnam conflict. In this section we inquire whether such a negotiation/arbitration process, once started, would have been completed successfully.

Recall that such a process consists of up to three steps. The first step consists of negotiation; if all issues are successfully resolved, the process ends there successfully. If not, the parties should express their remaining disagreements as succinctly as possible, so as to limit as much as possible the scope of the issues to be arbitrated. The second step would then be for the parties to select (negotiate on) arbitrator(s) and the terms of reference. The final step would be for the arbitrator(s) to decide on a solution.

In the Vietnam dispute, it is clear that the United States would have had to yield on one of its demands, namely the maintenance of South Vietnam under the existing anticommunist government. For one thing, the Vietnamese Communists (this term is here meant to include both the North Vietnamese and the NLF) had made it amply clear that they would prefer an indefinitely long war, achievable unilaterally, to that solution. (An arbitrated solution must not be of less utility to any of the parties than what it can achieve unilaterally.) Within that constraint, there was a range of solutions which, minus the war that occurred, would have been better for everybody. In particular, since the Vietnamese Communists anticipated a longer war than actually occurred (Karnow 1983, 18), the United States, apart from avoiding the war, could probably have attained a better arrangement in Vietnam than that which ultimately occurred (seizure of South Vietnam by Communist forces). The North Vietnamese negotiating position in 1964 was that U.S. forces should withdraw, that the affairs of the South must be arranged by the people of the South with the NLF playing a major role, and that the South could have neutrality with no hurry about reunification, this being a matter for negotiation without military pressures between North and South (Kahin 1986, 213–14).

The issues for negotiation/arbitration would thus have included how the government of South Vietnam should be determined, presumably through elections (how supervised?), and the role of the NLF relative to that of the other factions in South Vietnam. This would have determined the degree of Communist influence in the new South Vietnam government, and whether and how long South Vietnam remained neutralized, relative to the risk (from the U.S. viewpoint) that South Vietnam could be absorbed into a unified Communist Vietnam. During the negotiation/ arbitration process, the United States would have learned (as we apparently did not in the actual conflict), that Vietnam's interests differed from those of the Soviet Union and especially of China (Karnow 1983, 32, 43), and that Vietnam would act independently once freed from the need of help in fighting the United States. Whether or not negotiations would by themselves have led to agreement or would have been preparation for the arbitration step, they should have led the United States to the realization that a Vietnam war would be long and costly (the Vietnamese Communists had always assumed this), and would have led the United States to appreciate that a Communist takeover of Vietnam would have led to the consequences that actually occurred, and not to a wider Communist takeover in Southeast Asia or elsewhere.

The dispute has thus been modeled as one where the cost of not reaching agreement is high, and where the change in payoff to either party due to the parameters remaining to be decided is relatively low. The parameters to be decided might have been the expected speed and completeness of transition from a separate neutralist South Vietnam to a unified Communist Vietnam, likely to pursue its own nationalist cause independently from the Soviet Union and China. The range of these parameters was immediate unification under the Communists (as actually happened) at one extreme, to a permanently neutralized separate South Vietnam at the other extreme, with the arbitrated solution somewhere in this range. For example (and only one example), an intermediate solution might have been a separate elected neutralist government of South Vietnam guaranteed for x years, with no military interference of any kind. How the governments of North and South Vietnam would then settle the issue of reunification x years hence could depend to some extent on intervening history.

The conditions for arbitration, if still necessary, would then have existed. The advantage of arbitration for both sides, relative to the war that actually occurred, would have been great, with correspondingly high motivation on both sides to agree on arbitrator(s) to put arbitration into effect. Surely, there would have been arbitrators to be found who were competent and unbiased (for example, U.N. Secretary General U Thant and the International Control Commission, which had been set up in 1954 for South Vietnam). A successful outcome of arbitration would have followed.

NOTES

CHAPTER 2

1.   The phrase "Nuclear war cannot be won and must never be fought" is in Ronald Reagan's address to the General Assembly on September 26, 1983 (reported in the New York *Times,* September 27, 1983, p. A16), in the joint U.S.–Soviet statement following the Geneva summit meeting in November 1985 (reported in the New York *Times,* November 22, 1985, section 1, p. 15), and in Mikhail Gorbachev, *Perestroika: New Thinking for Our Country and the World* (New York: Harper & Row, 1987), p. 226.

2.   Such a scenario is also discussed by Stephen H. Unger in "The Demise of Defense," *IEEE Technology and Society Magazine* 2, no. 3 (September 1983): 3–10, 23.

3.   The theory of nuclear winter is that the dust and smoke from the explosion of many nuclear weapons would largely prevent the sun's energy from reaching the earth's surface, resulting in so extensive a decrease in temperature that human life and that of other species might become extinct. An annotated bibliography is given in Lutishoor Salisbury, "Nuclear Winter: Environmental Consequences of Nuclear War," *IEEE*

Technology and Society Magazine 6, no. 1 (March 1987): 21–28. A short review of nuclear winter papers is also given in Melvin Klerer, "The Nuclear Winter Hypothesis: Implications for Scientific Credibility," *IEEE Technology and Society Magazine* 4, no. 1 (March 1985): 16–18.

4. For a more detailed analysis of ballistic missile defense, see Robert M. Bowman, "Star Wars and Security," *IEEE Technology and Society Magazine* 4, no. 4 (December 1985): 2–13.

CHAPTER 3

1. A general reference to the various forms of dispute resolution, with an extensive bibliography, is Stephen B. Goldberg, Eric D. Green, and Frank E. A. Sander, *Dispute Resolution* (Boston: Little, Brown and Co., 1985).

2. Decomposition of negotiating problems into logical elements, and computerized search for good combinations is proposed by Vadim B. Lukov, Victor M. Sergeev, and Ivan G. Tyulin, "Reflective Model of Negotiations Process," *IEEE Technology and Society Magazine* 3, no. 2 (June 1984): 20–27.

3. Some court-ordered processes which are non-voluntary and non-binding are also called arbitration, but this nomenclature confuses the distinction between arbitration and mediation.

4. In addition to Goldberg, *Dispute Resolution,* cited in Note 1, see James F. Henry and Jethro K. Lieberman, *The Manager's Guide to Resolving Legal Disputes: Better Results Without Litigation* (New York: Harper & Row, 1985), for dispute resolution involving corporations, and Lawrence Suskind and Jeffrey Cruikshank, *Breaking the Impasse: Consensual Approaches to Resolving Public Disputes* (New York: Basic Books, 1987), for public interest disputes.

5. Christopher W. Moore, *The Mediation Process: Practical Strategies for Resolving Conflict* (San Francisco: Jossey-Bass, 1986), provides detailed procedures and techniques that negotiators can use, as well as an extensive bibliography.

6. Ibid., pp. 34–35, 39–43.

7. The Law of the Sea was not approved by the United States, in part because the U.S. administration had changed. See James K. Sebenius, *Negotiating the Law of the Sea* (Cambridge, MA: Harvard University Press, 1984), p. 71.

CHAPTER 4

1. R. Duncan Luce and Howard Raiffa, *Games and Decisions* (New York: John Wiley & Sons, 1957). More recent references include Martin Shubik, *Game Theory in the Social Sciences: Concepts and Solutions* (Cambridge, MA: MIT Press, 1982); Alvin E. Roth, ed., *Game Theoretic Models of Bargaining* (New York and Cambridge: Cambridge University Press, 1985); and Charles M. Benjamin and Charles A. Powell, eds., "Special Issue: Game Theory," *Peace and Change* 13 (1988).

2. Luce and Raiffa, *Games and Decisions,* pp. 71–72.

3. The claim is generally made that game theory provides the players with strategies that are rational. The term "rational" is hard to define; it usually means that it is the strategy that the proposer recommends.

4. For example, in Anatol Rapoport, "Games," *Peace and Change* 13 (1988): 38.

5. Anatol Rapoport, "Debates," *Peace and Change* 13 (1988): 59.

CHAPTER 5

1. Anatol Rapoport, "Games," pp. 18–42, reports that there are about 3,000 papers on the Prisoner's Dilemma; also provides a short history of the game.

2. Some analysts try to get around this dilemma by means of a theory of imitation. It is advantageous to be mistaken for a cooperator, such as a TIT FOR TAT player, so each player pretends temporarily to be a cooperator, and this results in uneasy cooperation for a while. See David M. Kreps et al., "Rational Cooperation in the Finitely Repeated Prisoner's Dilemma," *J. Economic Theory* 27 (1982): 245–52. A description of this approach is also given in Alvin E. Roth, ed., *Game Theoretic Models of Bargaining* (New York and Cambridge: Cambridge University Press, 1985), pp. 35–36.

3. Robert M. Axelrod, *The Evolution of Cooperation* (New York: Basic Books, 1984). (A summary of this work is given by Douglas R. Hofstadter in "Metamagical Themas: Computer Tournaments of the Prisoner's Dilemma Suggest How Cooperation Evolves," *Scientific American,* May 1983: 16–26, and also in *Metamagical Themas: Questing for the Essence of Mind and Pattern* [New York: Basic Books, 1985], pp. 715–34.)

4. Such a result is reported by Hofstadter in *Scientific American,* May 1983: 25–26, and in *Metamagical Themas,* p. 728.

5. For example, in Ulrich Mueller, "Optimal Retaliation for Optimal Cooperation," *J. Conflict Resolution* 31, no. 4 (December 1987): 692–724, TIT FOR TAT performance appeared undeservedly deficient because the unmodified, noise-vulnerable version of TIT FOR TAT was used.

6. In an experiment conducted by Douglas R. Hofstadter (*Metamagical Themas,* pp. 739–55) with 20 "rational" subjects, 14 defected and only 6 cooperated.

7. Robert H. Frank, *Passions Within Reason: The Strategic Role of the Emotions* (New York: W. W. Norton and Co., 1988) pp. 137–43. The PD payoff matrix in the experiment was $S = 0, P = \$1, R = \$2, T = \$3$.

CHAPTER 6

1. If there are more than two potential bidders, it is the first bidder who should apply the sanctions. It is (s)he that stands to gain if deterrence is successful, and it is (s)he who has a second-high bid at risk.

CHAPTER 7

1. For examples of noncompetitive games, see Alfie Kohn, *No-Contest: The Case Against Competition* (Boston: Houghton Mifflin, 1986), pp. 93–95; Terry Orlick, *The Cooperative Sports and Games Book* (New York: Pantheon Books, 1978) and *The Second Cooperative Sports and Games Book* (New York: Pantheon Books, 1982); and Family Pastimes Sales Catalog, R. R. 4, Perth, Ontario, Canada K7H 3C6. These sources recommend replacing competitive games with cooperative games; Kohn goes further and argues that all competition is inherently destructive.

CHAPTER 8

1. Scrabble crossword game is a game manufactured by the Selchow & Righter Company, which recently became a division of the Milton Bradley Company. The Scrabble literature includes Derryn Hinch, *The Scrabble Book* (New York: Mason/Charter,

1976) and Drue K. Conklin, *The Official Scrabble Player Handbook* (New York: Hamony Books/Crown, 1974, 1976). There is an active tournament organization, Scrabble Players, which publishes Scrabble Players News, Box 700, Greenport, NY 11944.

2. The following is a brief description of the conventional Scrabble crossword game:

The game is played on a board consisting of 15 x 15 squares. There are 100 letter tiles from which 7 are blindly taken by each player and placed on a rack concealed from the other players. At each turn, a player places any or all of his/her 7 tiles in a single row or column on the board, so that a single word results, left to right or top to bottom, either from those tiles alone or in combination with one or more tiles already there. Any touching letters in the perpendicular direction must also form words in that direction, crossword style. Acceptable words are those contained in an agreed-on dictionary. Except for the first word, which must be through the center square of the board, any new word must touch an existing word (horizontally or vertically) in at least one place.

The letters on the 100 tiles are roughly in proportion to their occurrence in the English language. A point value from 1 to 10 is also indicated on each tile, higher values being used for more difficult-to-place letters (Q and Z being each worth 10, and J and X each worth 8). Two blank wild-card tiles worth 0 are included. A player scores the sum total of the point values of all the letters of all new or changed words formed at a turn.

The board contains double letter, triple letter, double word, and triple word squares. A player who places a letter on such a square obtains the indicated premium for each word involved. For example, if X (value 8) is placed on a triple letter square, forming OX in one direction and AX in the other, the score would be 48 for the X, appearing in two words, plus 1 for the O and 1 for the A. The premiums apply in combination, so that if in a turn tiles are placed on a triple letter square and a double word square, the score for the tile placed on the triple letter square for the word through the double word square will be 6 times the value indicated on the tile. If a word is formed covering two triple word squares, the total score for that word is multiplied by 9. (Since triple letter squares are 8 letters apart, this is a rare event requiring at least one previously placed intervening letter.) One facet of good Scrabble play is to place high-score letters where multiples apply. There is a 50-point bonus for playing 7 tiles in a single turn.

After a turn, the rack is restocked to 7 letters, to the extent that there are letters left in the stock. Instead of placing letters on the board, a player may pass a turn (but not more than twice in succession) and discard, unrevealed, any number of his/her tiles, replace them with an equal number blindly from stock, and finally return the discarded tiles to the stock. This may be done only so long as there are more than 7 letters left in stock. Each player gets a turn in rotation. The game ends when the stock is exhausted and one player has used all his/her letters, or no player can place any more letters. Each player's score is reduced by the point value of his/her unplayed letters, and the player, if any, who used all his/her letters receives the point value of all the unplayed letters. The player with the highest score wins.

3. For example, "Master Monty Plays Scrabble," Timeless Expectation, P.O. Box 1180, Fairfield, IA 52556.

4. The Axelrod tournaments, described in Chapter 5, Section III, were not conducted in the way recommended in Chapter 8, but were round-robin tournaments with simple summation scoring. This scoring apparently did not cause any problems, which may be due to the fact that in iterated PD, a retaliatory move (playing D) is also a good security move. However, with simple round-robin scoring, TIT FOR TAT could be beaten by a strategy N in a round-robin match where TIT FOR TAT is partnered with itself and with N, and N is partnered with itself and with TIT FOR TAT. Strategy N is the original TIT FOR TAT (stated in Section III of Chapter 5) except for the following modification when play has been all C until move n:

1. On move n, play D
2. On move $n+1$, play the opposite of whatever partner played on move n.

When N is partnered with itself, each partner would play D once, costing N two points with respect to TIT FOR TAT playing against itself. When N and TIT FOR TAT are partners, N would score 5 more points than TIT FOR TAT on move n; thereafter, play would be all D. Hence N would win the tournament by 3 points. N would win not because it is a superior non-zero-sum strategy, but because it takes advantage of a flaw in the scoring.

CHAPTER 9

1. The nonplayer who desires a quick introduction to bridge is probably better off with the bridge section in a game book such as Tom Ainslee, *Ainslee's Complete Hoyle* (New York: Simon and Schuster, 1975), than a book devoted to beginner bridge.

CHAPTER 11

1. See, for example, Amartya K. Sen, *Collective Choice and Social Welfare* (San Francisco: Holden-Day, 1970), for a discussion of the social welfare function. A recent update of welfare economics is given by Peter Hammond in Chapter 13, "Welfare Economics," of *Issues in Contemporary Microeconomics and Welfare*, ed. George R. Feiwel (Albany, NY: State University of New York Press, 1985).

2. Many classical game theory results derive from the Nash solution to the bargaining problem. The Nash solution in turn depends on the assumption that utility is not intercomparable, which is stated more formally as that multiplication of the utilities of one of the players by a constant shall not change the bargaining solution. This assumption, together with Pareto optimality, symmetry, and independence of irrelevant alternatives, leads to the Nash solution, namely that the one and only outcome in a bargaining encounter between two players that satisfies the above assumptions is the one that maximizes the product of the utilities of the two players with respect to the utilities if no bargaining agreement is reached. This is so because the only function not influenced by change in relative utility scales is the product. For a more complete development of the Nash bargaining solution, see Chapter 6 of R. Duncan Luce and Howard Raiffa, *Games and Decisions* (New York: John Wiley & Sons, 1957). The large role that this result plays in game theory is evident from the remainder of that book. The original paper by J. F. Nash is "The Bargaining Problem," *Econometrica* 18 (1950): 155–62.

The following differences between utility-product maximization as used in classical game theory and as used in this book for welfare maximization should be noted:

1. The extension from the utility product of two players to that of n players (equation 11-3) is usually not made in classical

game theory.
2. Since non-intercomparability of utilities is such an extreme assumption, the many classical game theory results that rest on this assumption must be suspect; on the other hand, utility product maximization is treated as an extreme case in Chapter 11 of this book.
3. Extensions of Nash bargaining results to more general games are usually based on what is cautioned against in Chapter 11, namely presuming reference utilities to be the lowest (most negative) available, far outside the Pareto optimal range.

3. A pioneering paper is Roger B. Myerson, "Incentive Compatibility and the Bargaining Problem," *Econometrica* 47 (1979): 61–73.

Myerson gives the following example: Two players must share the cost of a project, such as the cost of paving a road which only these two use. The project would cost $100 (pre–1980 prices!), and the two players have called in an arbitrator to help them divide the cost. It is known that the project would be worth $90 to player X, but its value to player Y depends on Y's type, which only Y knows for sure. If Y is type 1, then the project would also be worth $90 to Y, but if Y is type 2 ("thinks old unpaved roads have rustic charm"), then the project would be worth only $30 to Y. The probability that Y is type 2 is 0.1. The arbitrator will ask Y to state Y's type, but it is known that Y will lie if that would be of benefit to Y.

The solution arrived at by Myerson is as follows:

If Y claims to be type 1, then the project should be produced for sure, with X paying $49.50 and Y paying $50.50.
If Y claims to be type 2, then the project should be produced only with probability 0.439, but if it is produced, X should pay the entire cost.

It is clear that Myerson's incentive compatible solution is inferior to what could be attained if Y could be relied upon to tell the truth, for it is beneficial to undertake the project, regardless of Y's type. The probability of not undertaking the project is needed in order to provide incentive for Y to admit being type 1 if Y is type 1, as otherwise it would always be advantageous for Y to claim to be type 2, and thus no information could be obtained from Y.

Without such information, the overall welfare, assumed by Myerson to be the exponentially weighted product $U_X U_{Y1}^{0.9} U_{Y2}^{0.1}$ of expected utilities, would be less than with Myerson's solution. For example, always charging Y less than \$30 would excessively reduce X's utility, and always charging Y more than \$30 would cause Y to decline the project whenever Y was type 2. Also, at or slightly below \$30, the gain to $Y2$, a Y who happens to be type 2, would be zero or very small.

Another reference on the theory of incentives is Feiwel, *Issues in Contemporary Microeconomics and Welfare.*

CHAPTER 12

1. Differing opinions have been expressed in the literature about the advantages, if any, of final offer arbitration. It depends on how the process is modeled. Two differing views are given by Steven J. Brams and Samuel Merrill, III, in "Equilibrium Strategies for Final-Offer Arbitration: There Is No Median Convergence," *Management Science* 29 (August 1983): 927–41, and Gerald Rabow in "Response to 'Equilibrium Strategies for Final-Offer Arbitration: There Is No Median Convergence'," *Management Science* 31 (March 1985): 374–75.

2. The question of whether and why a process using arbitrators selected by disputants should produce different results than direct issue bargaining has been considered in the game theory literature, for example by Vincent P. Crawford, "The Role of Arbitration and the Theory of Incentives," in *Game Theoretic Models of Bargaining,* Alvin E. Roth, ed. (New York and Cambridge: Cambridge University Press, 1985), pp. 363–90, particularly pp. 370–71.

My view is that the most significant reason why bargaining over arbitrator selection differs from issue bargaining is that the disputants cannot model real arbitrators well enough to know in sufficient detail or with sufficient confidence how the inclusion of arbitrators has transformed the original "game." Hence, bargaining over arbitrator selection is a different game, and for the reasons mentioned in the body of Chapter 12 one that is easier to come to agreement on than the original dispute. (Even if arbitrator selection were to turn out to be no easier than issue negotiation, an arbitration alternative would provide two shots at settlement rather than one, since the negotiation situations would be different; after issue negotiation has been tried and failed, arbitrator selection could be tried.) Another way in which the arbitrator selection "game" differs from the original dispute is that the number of decision alternatives in the arbitrator selection game, namely the number of available arbitrators, differs in general from the number of possible solutions to the original dispute.

3. There has been a considerable mount of arbitration of public international law disputes (as distinct from transnational commercial disputes, where arbitration is now fairly routine). The first recorded case of international arbitration occurred during the third millenium B.C. in Mesopotamia (see Gregory A. Raymond, *Conflict Resolution and the Structure of the State System: An Analysis of Arbitrative Settlements* [Montclair, N.J.: Allenheld Osmun, 1980)], p. 1.) A. M. Stuyt in *Survey of International Arbitration 1794–1970* (Leiden, The Netherlands: A. W. Sijthoff, 1972) lists about 500 arbitrations between national states in the period 1794 to 1970; 117 of them involved the United States. The latter include, for example, boundary disputes with Mexico and with Great Britain (regarding Alaska), ship sinking and ship seizure disputes (e.g., with Great Britain, Canada, and Russia), claims for injuries and losses suffered by Americans in foreign countries (e.g., Panama, Guatemala, and Haiti), and the Alabama case in which Great Britain had to pay a $15.5 million award to the United States for having built a warship for the Southern States in the Civil War.

4. Arbitration for ethnic and territory problems is recommended in István Bibó, *The Paralysis of International Institutions and the Remedies: A Study of Self-Determination, Concord Among the Major Powers, and Political Arbitration* (New York: John Wiley & Sons, 1976). Bibó refers to such arbitration as international political arbitration, as distinguished from regular international arbitration, referred to in Note 3.

5. George Kahin, *Intervention: How America Became Involved in Vietnam* (New York: Alfred A. Knopf, 1986), pp. 88–92.

6. Ibid., pp. 213–14.

7. For example, a July 1965 estimate in the U.S. Defense Department gave only a 50 percent probability of success by 1968 with the introduction of 200,000 to 400,000 plus U.S. troops (Kahin, *Intervention*, p. 357).

8. Richard B. Bilder, "Some Limitations of Adjudication as an International Dispute Settlement Technique," in *Resolving*

*Transnational Disputes through International Arbitration: Sixth
Sokol Colloquium, 1982,* Thomas E. Carbonneau, ed.
(Charlottesville: University Press of Virginia, 1984), pp. 3–14.

9. Dean Rusk, "The Role and Problems of Arbitration with
Respect to Political Disputes," in Carbonneau, *Resolving
Transnational Disputes,* pp. 15–20.

10. A contrary opinion needs to be addressed here, namely
that of John G. Stoessinger in *Why Nations Go to War,* 2d ed.
(New York: St. Martin's Press, 1978), where on p. 227 he
concludes

> The case material reveals that perhaps the most important
> single precipitating factor in the outbreak of war is
> misperception. . . . There is a remarkable consistency in
> the self-images of most national leaders on the brink of
> war. Each confidently expects victory after a brief and
> triumphant campaign.

There are several reasons why matters should be
different once arbitration is utilized. One thing arbitrators need
to do is analyze carefully the expected result if an agreement is
not reached and a unilateral solution (war) is attempted. This
analysis would, of course, be extensively discussed with all
parties to the dispute so as to reduce misperceptions both by the
arbitrator and by the disputing parties. Thus, the arbitration
process itself will reduce the misperceptions which can contribute
to the development of a war.

Recent lessons, that war against even relatively small
nations can go very badly, should further help overcome
misperceptions about easy victory. After the United States'
experience in Vietnam and the Soviet Union's experience in
Afghanistan, the risk and cost of any war should be apparent to
any decision maker. And hardly anyone misperceives the
outcome of nuclear war.

11. This explanation is suggested in Bibó, *The Paralysis of
International Institutions.*

12. Benjamin B. Ferencz and Ken Keyes, Jr., *Planethood:
The Key to Your Survival and Prosperity* (Coos Bay, OR: Vision
Books, 1988), p. 48.

13. Ibid., pp. 55–74.

14. Grenville Clark and Louis Sohn, *World Peace through
World Law* (Cambridge, MA: Harvard University Press, 1985,

1963, 1966), is a book-length proposal for world government.

15. See, for example, Grenville Clark and Louis Sohn, *Introduction to World Peace through World Law*, rev. 1984 ed. (Chicago: World Without War Publications), pp. 27–32.

CHAPTER 13

1. The case of, and means for, conversion are presented by John E. Ullmann, "Conversion of the Military-Industrial Sector," *IEEE Technology and Society Magazine* 3, no. 3 (September 1984): 3–9, and Kevin J. Cassidy, "Arms Control and the Home Front: Planning for the Conversion of Military Production to Civilian Manufacturing," *Peace and Change* 14, no. 1 (January 1989): 46–64.

I would like to add one friendly amendment to these papers. They state that in order to compete successfully in the civilian economy, defense contractors must become more cost-conscious and hence learn how to market products to multiple consumers. I think that this is viewing conversion too narrowly. Many of the things that society needs doing, and that are now preempted by military expenditures, are tasks for the benefit of the public. Here the costs ought often not be primary and the work can be procured by government, just as in the case of military systems. A partial list includes space exploration and other science projects, protection and restoration of the environment, catchup on the maintenance of our infrastructure, making adequate medical and long-term nursing care available to everybody, educating all to the limits of their ability, research to not only overcome present diseases, but to anticipate and prevent crises such as AIDS in the future, and a fundamental attack on the problems of addictions of all kinds leading to their understanding, prevention, and cure. It might be well for government to shift much of the reductions in military expenditures, when they occur, toward the satisfaction of such societal needs, in a way that makes use of the freed-up workers and their talents.

BIBLIOGRAPHY

Ainslee, Tom. *Ainslee's Complete Hoyle.* New York: Simon and Schuster, 1975.

Axelrod, Robert M. *The Evolution of Cooperation.* New York: Basic Books, 1984.

Ball, George W. *The Past Has Another Pattern: Memoirs.* New York: W. W. Norton and Co., 1982.

Benjamin, Charles M., and Charles A. Powell, eds. "Special Issue: Game Theory." *Peace and Change* 13 (1988).

Bibó, István. *The Paralysis of International Institutions and the Remedies: A Study of Self-Determination, Concord Among the Major Powers, and Political Arbitration.* New York: John Wiley & Sons, 1976.

Bilder, Richard B. "Some Limitations of Adjudication as an International Dispute Settlement Technique." In *Resolving*

Transnational Disputes through International Arbitration: Sixth Sokol Colloquium, 1982, edited by Thomas E. Carbonneau, pp. 3–14. Charlottesville: University Press of Virginia, 1984.

Bowman, Robert M. "Star Wars and Security." *IEEE Technology and Society Magazine* 4, no. 4 (December 1985): 2–13.

Brams, Steven J., and Samuel Merrill, III. "Equilibrium Strategies for Final-Offer Arbitration: There Is No Median Convergence." *Management Science* 29 (August 1983): 927–41.

Carbonneau, Thomas E., ed. *Resolving Transnational Disputes through International Arbitration: Sixth Sokol Colloquium, 1982.* Charlottesville: University Press of Virginia, 1984.

Cassidy, Kevin J. "Arms Control and the Home Front: Planning for the Conversion of Military Production to Civilian Manufacturing." *Peace and Change* 14, no. 1 (January 1989): 46–64.

Clark, Grenville, and Louis Sohn. *World Peace through World Law.* Cambridge, MA: Harvard University Press, 1958, 1963, 1966.

____. *Introduction to World Peace through World Law.* Revised 1984 ed. Chicago: World Without War Publications.

Conklin, Drue K. *The Official Scrabble Player Handbook.* New York: Harmony Books/Crown, 1974, 1976.

Crawford, Vincent P. "The Role of Arbitration and the Theory of Incentives." In *Game Theoretic Models of Bargaining,* edited by Alvin E. Roth, pp. 363–90. New York and Cambridge: Cambridge University Press, 1985.

Feiwel, George R., ed. *Issues in Contemporary Microeconomics and Welfare.* Albany, NY: State University of New York Press, 1985.

Ferencz, Benjamin B., and Ken Keyes, Jr. *Planethood: The Key to Your Survival and Prosperity.* Coos Bay, OR: Vision Books, 1988.

Fisher, Roger, and William Ury. *Getting to Yes: Negotiating Agreement Without Giving In.* New York: Penguin Books, 1983.

Frank, Robert H. *Passions Within Reason: The Strategic Role of the Emotions.* New York: W. W. Norton and Co., 1988.

Goldberg, Stephen B., Eric D. Green, and Frank E. A. Sander. *Dispute Resolution.* Boston: Little, Brown and Co., 1985.

Gorbachev, Mikhail. *Perestroika: New Thinking for our Country and the World.* New York: Harper & Row, 1987.

Hammond, Peter. "Welfare Economics." In *Issues in Contemporary Microeconomics and Welfare,* edited by George R. Feiwel, pp. 405–34. Albany, NY: State University of New York Press, 1985.

Henry, James F., and Jethro K. Lieberman. *The Manager's Guide to Resolving Legal Disputes: Better Results Without Litigation.* New York: Harper & Row, 1985.

Hinch, Derryn, *The Scrabble Book.* New York: Mason/Charter, 1976.

Hofstadter, Douglas R. "Metamagical Themas: Computer Tournaments of the Prisoner's Dilemma Suggest How Cooperation Evolves." *Scientific American* (May 1983): 16–26.

_____. *Metamagical Themas: Questing for the Essence of Mind and Pattern.* New York: Basic Books, 1985.

Kahin, George M. *Intervention: How America Became Involved in Vietnam.* New York: Alfred A. Knopf, 1986.

Karnow, Stanley. *Vietnam: A History.* New York: Viking Press, 1983.

Klerer, Melvin. "The Nuclear Winter Hypothesis: Implications for Scientific Credibility." *IEEE Technology and Society Magazine* 4, no. 1 (March 1985): 16–18.

Kohn, Alfie. *No-Contest: The Case Against Competition*. Boston: Houghton Mifflin, 1986.

Kreps, David M., et al. "Rational Cooperation in the Finitely Repeated Prisoner's Dilemma." *Journal of Economic Theory* 27 (1982): 245–52.

Luce, Duncan R., and Howard Raiffa. *Games and Decisions*. New York: John Wiley & Sons, 1957.

Lukov, Vadim B., Victor M. Sergeev, and Ivan G. Tyulin. "Reflective Model of Negotiations Process." *IEEE Technology and Society Magazine* 3, no. 2 (June 1984): 20–27.

Moore, Christopher W. *The Mediation Process: Practical Strategies for Resolving Conflict*. San Francisco: Jossey-Bass, 1986.

Mueller, Ulrich. "Optimal Retaliation for Optimal Cooperation." *Journal of Conflict Resolution* 31, no. 4 (December 1987): 692–724.

Myerson, Roger B. "Incentive Compatibility and the Bargaining Problem." *Econometrica* 47 (1979): 61–73.

Nash, J. F. "The Bargaining Problem." *Econometrica* 18 (1950): 155–62.

O'Neill, Barry. "International Escalation and the Dollar Auction." *Journal of Conflict Resolution* 30, no. 1 (March 1986): 33–50.

Orlick, Terry. *The Cooperative Sports and Games Book*. New York: Pantheon Books, 1978.

____. *The Second Cooperative Sports and Games Book*. New York: Pantheon Books, 1982.

Rabow, Gerald. "Response to 'Equilibrium Strategies for Final-Offer Arbitration: There is No Median Convergence'." *Management Science* 31 (March 1985): 374–75.

____. "Arbitration as a Means for Resolving Major International Disputes." *IEEE Technology and Society Magazine* 6, no. 3 (September 1987): 11–16.

____. "The Cooperative Edge: New versions of Scrabble, bridge, and basketball help teach us the advantages of cooperation in play and real life." *Psychology Today* (January 1988): 54–58. (a)

____. "The Social Implications of Non-Zero-Sum Games." *IEEE Technology and Society Magazine* 7, no. 1 (March 1988): 12–18. (b)

Raiffa, Howard. *The Art and Science of Negotiation.* Cambridge, MA: Harvard University Press, Belknap Press, 1982.

Rapoport, Anatol. "Games." *Peace and Change* 13 (1988): 18–43.

____. "Debates." *Peace and Change* 13 (1988): 44–62.

Raymond, Gregory A. *Conflict Resolution and the Structure of the State System: An Analysis of Arbitrative Settlements.* Montclair, NJ: Allenheld Osmun, 1980.

Roth, Alvin E., ed. *Game Theoretic Models of Bargaining.* New York and Cambridge: Cambridge University Press, 1985.

Rusk, Dean. "The Role and Problems of Arbitration with Respect to Political Disputes," in *Resolving Transnational Disputes through International Arbitration: Sixth Sokol Colloquium, 1982,* edited by Thomas E. Carbonneau, pp. 15–20. Charlottesville: University Press of Virginia, 1984.

Salisbury, Lutishoor. "Nuclear Winter: Environmental Consequences of Nuclear War." *IEEE Technology and Society Magazine* 6, no. 1 (March 1987): 21–28.

Sebenius, James K. *Negotiating the Law of the Sea.* Cambridge, MA: Harvard University Press, 1984.

Sen, Amartya K. *Collective Choice and Social Welfare.* San Francisco: Holden-Day, 1970.

Shubik, Martin. *Game Theory in the Social Sciences: Concepts and Solutions.* Cambridge, MA: MIT Press, 1982.

Stoessinger, John G. *Why Nations Go to War.*, 2d ed. New York: St. Martin's Press, 1978.

Stuyt, A. M. *Survey of International Arbitration 1794–1970.* Leiden, The Netherlands: A. W. Sijthoff, 1972.

Susskind, Lawrence, and Jeffrey Cruikshank. *Breaking the Impasse: Consensual Approaches to Resolving Public Disputes.* New York: Basic Books, 1987.

Tuchman, Barbara W. *The March of Folly: From Troy to Vietnam.* Boston: Hall and Co., 1984.

Ullmann, John E. "Conversion of the Military-Industrial Sector." *IEEE Technology and Society Magazine* 3, no. 3 (September 1984): 3–9.

Unger, Stephen H. "The Demise of Defense." *IEEE Technology and Society Magazine* 2, no. 3 (September 1983): 3–10, 23.

Von Neumann, John, and Oskar Morgenstern. *Theory of Games and Economic Behavior.* Princeton: Princeton University Press, 1944, 1947.

INDEX

ABM (Anti-Ballistic Missile)
Treaty, 12
alternative dispute resolution
(ADR), 23–24
arbitration, x, 20, 26–28;
advantages of final offer,
175n; characteristics of,
27; comparison with
mediation, 23; for ethnic
and territory problems,
176n; facilitation of
availability of acceptable
arbitrators, 131–34; of
major international
disputes, 4–5, 121–44;
overcoming perceived
limitations on, 134–38;
and rationality, 137;
reluctance in, 138; scheme

in, of major international
disputes, 7; vis-a-vis world
government, 138–44. *See
also* International dispute
arbitration
Arbitration Institute, 131–32
arbitrator: facilitation of
availability of, 131–34;
performance of, 126–27;
selection of, 125–26;
arms control, 146–49
arms control agreement
agendas, 149
arms reduction, 127–28
atmospheric testing of nuclear
weapons, 148–49
Axelrod, Robert M., 48, 49
Axelrod's tournaments, 102,
172n

ABOUT THE AUTHOR

GERALD RABOW has spent his career in systems engineering with IT&T, Otis Elevator Research Center, and AT&T Bell Laboratories. He has become increasingly engaged in research and writing on applying systems engineering approaches toward the solution of societal problems, especially that of attaining peace. He is an officer and founding member of the IEEE Society on Social Implications of Technology.